Neptune Frost

TIMECODES

A book series exploring individual movies minute by minute.

Series Editors
Nicholas Rombes, University of Detroit Mercy, USA
Nadine Boljkovac, University of Colorado, USA

Advisory Board
Paweł Frelik (University of Warsaw, Poland)
Andrew Gallix (Independent Scholar, France)
Colleen Kennedy-Karpat (Bilkent University, Turkey)
Scott Macaulay (*Filmmaker Magazine* co-founder, USA)
Shiva Moghanloo (Independent Scholar, Iran)
Björn Sonnenberg-Schrank (Heinrich Heine University Düsseldorf, Germany)
Steven Shaviro (Wayne State University, USA)
Constantine Verevis (Monash University, Australia)

Also in the Series:
Gerry: Movies Minute by Minute, by Nicholas Rombes
BlacKkKlansman: Movies Minute by Minute, by **Alex Zamalin**
Twin Peaks: The Return, Part 8, by Jeff Wood

Neptune Frost

Movies Minute by Minute

Steven Shaviro

BLOOMSBURY ACADEMIC
NEW YORK • LONDON • OXFORD • NEW DELHI • SYDNEY

BLOOMSBURY ACADEMIC
Bloomsbury Publishing Inc, 1359 Broadway, New York, NY 10018, USA
Bloomsbury Publishing Plc, 50 Bedford Square, London, WC1B 3DP, UK
Bloomsbury Publishing Ireland, 29 Earlsfort Terrace, Dublin 2, D02 AY28, Ireland

BLOOMSBURY, BLOOMSBURY ACADEMIC and the Diana logo are trademarks of
Bloomsbury Publishing Plc

First published in the United States of America 2026

Copyright © Steven Shaviro, 2026

Cover design: Eleanor Rose
Cover image © Freya Betts

All rights reserved. No part of this publication may be: i) reproduced or transmitted in any form, electronic or mechanical, including photocopying, recording or by means of any information storage or retrieval system without prior permission in writing from the publishers; or ii) used or reproduced in any way for the training, development or operation of artificial intelligence (AI) technologies, including generative AI technologies. The rights holders expressly reserve this publication from the text and data mining exception as per Article 4(3) of the Digital Single Market Directive (EU) 2019/790.

Bloomsbury Publishing Inc does not have any control over, or responsibility for, any third-party websites referred to or in this book. All internet addresses given in this book were correct at the time of going to press. The author and publisher regret any inconvenience caused if addresses have changed or sites have ceased to exist, but can accept no responsibility for any such changes.

Library of Congress Cataloging-in-Publication Data
Names: Shaviro, Steven author
Title: Neptune Frost : movies minute by minute / Steven Shaviro.
Description: New York : Bloomsbury Academic, 2026. |
Series: Timecodes | Includes bibliographical references and index.
Identifiers: LCCN 2025024884 | ISBN 9798765161913 hardback |
ISBN 9798765161906 paperback | ISBN 9798765161937 pdf |
ISBN 9798765161944 epub Subjects: LCSH: Neptune Frost (Motion picture) | LCGFT:
Film criticism Classification: LCC PN1997.2.N47 S43 2026 | DDC 791.43/72—dc23/
eng/20250623 LC record available at https://lccn.loc.gov/2025024884

ISBN: HB: 979-8-7651-6191-3
PB: 979-8-7651-6190-6
ePDF: 979-8-7651-6193-7
eBook: 979-8-7651-6194-4

Series: Timecodes

Typeset by Deanta Global Publishing Services, Chennai, India
Printed and bound in the United States of America

For product safety related questions contact productsafety@bloomsbury.com.

To find out more about our authors and books visit www.bloomsbury.com
and sign up for our newsletters.

For Adah and Roxanne and in memory of Vivian Kerman and William Zukerman

CONTENTS

Preface viii

Minutes 1–101 1

Works Cited 95
Index 101

PREFACE

She considered tea and coffee abominable for their bloody history, but drank them anyway. You can avoid blood diamonds relatively easily but you can't avoid coffee. And obviously I can't escape tantalum capacitors either; ethical consumption is an oxymoron.

VAJRA CHANDRASEKERA

Neptune Frost is a 2021 film that resists simple description. Perhaps it is best categorized as an Afrofuturist musical, though it has little in common with *The Wiz* (Sidney Lumet, 1978), the movie that most obviously fits this designation. *Neptune Frost* splits the difference between being an auteurist art movie and a genre film, as well as between being an American film and an African one. It is codirected by the African American rapper, performance artist, and poet Saul Williams and the Rwandan cinematographer Anisia Uzeyman. Williams wrote the screenplay and composed the music; Uzeyman photographed the movie. The film was shot in Rwanda and edited in Los Angeles by the Indian American editor Anisha Acharya. *Neptune Frost* is a polyglot film, with dialogue in five languages: Kinyarwanda, Kirundi, Swahili, French, and English. The actors switch fluently among all these tongues. There are English subtitles, which are the source of everything that I quote here.

Neptune Frost spans multiple genres and works by the way that it fuses them together. In the first place, it is a political movie with a conscious message. It offers us a stark account of oppression, together with a fugitive, yet extravagant, counter-vision of potential liberation. The movie envisages radical political change or Black liberation, not only in its explicit narrative but equally so in its very look and feel. Its visual and sonic textures seem at once carefully grounded and unearthly. Everything we hear and see is rooted in our present historical moment, but also pushes beyond it. From this point of view, I am reminded of Jean Renoir's great film for the French Popular Front, *The Crime of Monsieur Lange* (1936), which similarly presents a utopian vision of liberation grounded in, but pushing beyond, a concrete historical situation and which fuses the story of a particular protagonist with that of a collective of workers.

In the second place, *Neptune Frost* is a science fiction movie. As theorists such as Raymond Williams (1978), Tom Moylan (2014/1986), and Fredric Jameson (2005) have all argued, in contemporary society the utopian imagination finds its most powerful expression in science fiction. This is certainly the case for *Neptune Frost*, which imagines a group of outlaw computer hackers setting up their own Temporary Autonomous Zone (Bey 2003) in the highland forest. Digitaria, as they call it, is a new community that offers refuge from oppression and within which they live self-reliantly. Here they both work and play. A lot of the time, we see them partying and dancing. But Digitaria is also an Archimedean point, from which they can intervene in, and struggle to overthrow, the capitalist world order. In its many dimensions, the film fulfills Ytasha L. Womack's canonical definition of Afrofuturism as "an intersection of imagination, technology, the future and liberation," seeking to "redefine culture and notions of Blackness for today and the future" (Womack 2013).

In the third place, alongside both anti-capitalist agitprop and Afrofuturist science fiction, *Neptune Frost* is a full-fledged musical. People often sing words that would be spoken as dialogue in a more conventional film. States of mind are translated into song and dance, together with joyously extravagant visualizations. The film imagines social transformation both in science-fictional terms and through the vectors of music and dance. *Neptune Frost* portrays the actualities of patriarchal, economic, and racial oppression; but it also gives us the vision and audition of a potential world that resists and stands apart from such formations of power.

Neptune Frost is especially suited for a minute-by-minute analysis because it is such a densely textured and resonant film. It offers us a particularly rich tapestry of images and sounds, the latter including speech, music, and singing, together with diegetic and non-diegetic noises. Although *Neptune Frost* may seem chaotic at first viewing, it actually has a fairly linear narrative. But this narrative is not, in itself, the movie's central concern. Rather, the narrative is a bare framework; multiple sensory and thematic elements are draped over it. With its lavish sounds and images, *Neptune Frost* expresses both gorgeous aestheticism and political resolve. And most importantly, it refuses to entertain any sense of a contradiction between these two dimensions.

Minutes 1–101

Minute 1

The first minute of the film is devoted to its company credits, with corporate logos mostly printed in white against an otherwise black screen. However, we do not see the title of the movie in this opening or any of the names of the cast or crew. *Neptune Frost* was released in the United States by Kino Lorber. But despite its mainstream distributor, the film has an unusual provenance. It was made outside of Hollywood, and indeed, outside of any of the usual systems of support for making films. *Neptune Frost* was initially funded by a crowdsourcing campaign on Kickstarter (Kickstarter 2018); I myself contributed $25 to its production, both because it sounded interesting and new, and because of my previous familiarity with the music and lyrics of Saul Williams. The Kickstarter campaign raised $196,000 in total; Williams then "used the fundraiser as leverage to raise more than $1 million in additional financing" (Vourlias 2021). This makes for an extraordinarily low-budget film by contemporary standards. Indeed, the filmmakers were still raising money even as the film was being shot (Vourlias 2021). Williams and Uzeyman originally envisaged *Neptune Frost* as "a stage play, a musical and as a graphic novel" (Chang 2022). But as their ambitions developed, they reconceived it in cinematic terms. In 2016, Williams released his album *Martyr Loser King*, with English-language songs that were subsequently translated into other languages and adapted for the movie. This title, the phrase "martyr loser king," is a transformation of the name "Martin Luther King" and comes up several times in the course of the movie. Also, the first two words of the phrase are modulated into *Matalusa*, which is the name of the film's secondary protagonist. Of course, Dr. Martin Luther King can himself be regarded as a martyr to the cause of equal rights for Black people, murdered as he was by a white supremacist. Dr. King might also be considered a "loser" in a certain ironic sense, for his political quest remains, to this day, an incomplete project. The last name, "King," however, implies sovereignty. *Neptune Frost* continually plays with multiple registers of meaning in this manner. Saul Williams subsequently released two additional albums that contain music for and from the film: *Encrypted and Vulnerable* (2019) and *Unanimous Goldmine* (2022). And the story also apparently exists in the form of a graphic novel, although this remains unpublished (Keogan 2022). Though Williams himself is American, the film as a whole is not. It was shot entirely in Rwanda. Aside from Williams himself, the cast and crew are all locals: either native Rwandans or refugees from Burundi. Williams explains that "although we always knew the story took place in Burundi, we could not go to Burundi because of political unrest. We knew that the Rwandan landscape was very similar to the Burundian landscape" (Gates 2022). Many of the actors are famous in their own countries, but they are not well-known in America or elsewhere in the world. In any case, the screen remains dark for the whole first minute of the film; but during the last few seconds of the credit sequence, we hear a premonitory electronic musical motif, together with a sort of chirping that evokes animal sounds. The motif will be repeated a number of times in the course of the film.

Minute 2

After the credits, the first actual shot of *Neptune Frost* is a close-up of a woman's face. When we first see her, she is looking away from us. But she quickly turns her head

FIGURE 1 Neptune Frost *directed by Saul Williams and Anisia Uzeyman* © *Kino Lorber 2021. All rights reserved.*

and stares directly into the camera, and therefore at us. The woman's glance is enigmatic, but also—as Jeremy Laughery puts it—"confrontative, resistive, and unafraid to contest the technologized gaze that threatens their identity, expression, and freedom from oppression throughout the film" (Laughery 2025). The woman has colorful dreadlocks and glittery eyeshadow; she wears a kind of headdress or mask with a horizontal mesh that encases her face. For now, this opening shot is a mystery; we do not yet know the woman's name, nor why she is looking at us in the way she does. We will soon learn that this is Neptune, the main protagonist of the film, in her female aspect (Cheryl Isheja). As the music swells up, the film cuts to a shot of the sky, with fair-weather clouds. Next comes a reverse shot, showing us the person who is looking up at the sky: this is a young man, Neptune in his male aspect (Elvis Ngabo aka "Bobo"). The camera hovers over him as he leans his head backward. Voice-over narration accompanies this shot, implying the inner monologue of the person whose face we see. But the voice is female. This is our first intimation of Neptune's intersexuality, conveyed in various ways, but most notably through the alternation of the male and female actors playing the same character. The film insists, right at the beginning, upon the wavering uncertainty of our most taken-for-granted binaries (here, male and female) and upon their capacity for metamorphosis. Williams speaks in an interview of "the desire to break the binary, to move beyond it, to reflect the spectrum of consciousness as we know and experience it on this planet" (Ngema 2022). The movie works by conflating and weaving together seemingly clashing images and sounds in order to convey a more complex reality. Here, Neptune's female inner voice, accompanying her outwardly male body, begins by saying that "I was born in my 23rd year." Her previous life was a fantasmatic one because war broke out just after her physical birth. Twenty-two years of continual destruction have separated Neptune's physical coming into existence from the present moment of experiential birth or rebirth: a process that will include a shifting of gender. The voice-over continues, with the narrator saying that her Aunt, who raised her, saw this time as already an "afterlife," rather than as a full and authentic form of existence. Nonetheless, throughout this time of suspension, or of not-quite-living, Neptune's Aunt "thanked God for every single day." For Neptune himself/herself, this "afterlife" precedes her birth, rather than succeeding her death. In any case, Neptune's Aunt persisted, and survived, in the face of continual violence and oppression. It is only now that she has finally passed; in this opening scene, we watch her funeral. The male Neptune straightens his head and looks forward as the camera pulls backward behind him. People are seated in a semicircle on the ground, facing a standing Christian pastor (Diogene Ntarindwa "Atome") who wears a priest's black shirt and white collar under a surprisingly garish purple jacket.

Minute 3

The pastor starts speaking, and everybody stands up. There is a shot-reverse shot sequence of glances exchanged between the preacher and the male Neptune, implying some sort of connection. But how well they know one another is not clear. The pastor speaks to everyone, addressing their collective loss. He orates entirely in clichéd religious formulas, telling the mourners that "our Auntie was a human being" and that "after this life, there is another life." This phrase has an ironic resonance, of which the speaker is evidently unaware. For the film will indeed follow Neptune to another life; but this new existence will not be an afterlife, but a fully material and worldly experience in the living present. The crowd responds to the preacher's words with a collective "Amen." The next shot points downward at the grave, as people start throwing dirt and flowers into it. The film then cuts to a striking reverse shot from the bottom of the grave. We hear the sound of dirt being tossed into the hole, which means that it is also tossed over the camera, obliterating any further view. But even before the dirt hits the lens, the camera lens is already covered, for the most part, by red flowers that were previously thrown into the grave. As happens so often throughout *Neptune Frost*, familiar formal structures—here the traditional shot/reverse shot alternation—are used for unconventional ends. For what is the point of view of a buried coffin? The film gives us, at least briefly, the perspective of the dead person. This suggests both an odd displacement, and yet—across this displacement—continuities that are never entirely broken. Neptune's Aunt, now deceased, represented home for him. Now that she is gone, Neptune is set adrift, alienated, reduced to a state of dereliction—but also thereby permitted, for the very first time, to become himself/herself. The voice-over continues, with the female Neptune telling us that, prior to her rebirth at the age of twenty-three, "I was a good boy . . . but my life was never quite mine."

Minute 4

Neptune's voice-over continues, but the scene shifts. We now see miners at work in an open pit, breaking up rocks, digging for coltan. Guards armed with rifles stand over the miners, continually exhorting them to work harder. Even as Africa has been systematically "underdeveloped" by the affluent countries of the Global North (Rodney 2008/1972), the continent still remains central to the world economy, as well as to its communication and control network. This is exemplified by coltan mining. Coltan is the most plenteous source of tantalum, an element needed for the manufacture of modern electronic and computing devices. Tantalum capacitors are "widely used in communications, aerospace and military industries, submarine cables, advanced electronic devices, civil appliances, televisions, and many other aspects" (Advanced Refractory Metals 2024). The Democratic Republic of Congo and Rwanda supply "approximately 67% of world production" of coltan, which is then sent to the more affluent countries of the Global North (Champion 2019). Burundi, just south of Rwanda and

FIGURE 2 Neptune Frost *directed by Saul Williams and Anisia Uzeyman* © Kino Lorber 2021. All rights reserved.

east of the Congo, is also an important source of the mineral (Ndanezerewe 2024). Coltan mining is a harsh and difficult process. The extraction of the mineral is "environmentally hazardous," and it involves the "systematic exploitation of workers," who toil under "dangerous working conditions" (Wikipedia 2024a). In the early twenty-first century, coltan mining has resulted in "large-scale environmental degradation, human rights abuses, violence and death" (Ojewale 2022). For these reasons, Saul Williams has described "coltan as cotton" (Burton 2022). He means that coltan plays an analogous role in our globalized system of manufacture today to that played by cotton in the world system prior to 1865. The historian Jim Powell notes that, before the American Civil War, "the cotton trade was by far Britain's largest industry," and "80% of the raw cotton for that trade came from the slave states of the southern USA" (Powell 2021). As Eric Williams famously argued long ago, the capitalist industrial system, grounded in wage labor, was only able to take off in Great Britain because of its reliance upon chattel slavery in the southern United States (1994/1944). Globalized, networked capitalism in the twenty-first century similarly relies upon an older style of exploitation, enacted in the coltan mine that *Neptune Frost* shows us. One of the workers, Tekno (Robert Ninteretse), dislodges a gleaming rock; he stops digging in order to hold it up in wonder. An armed guard immediately bashes Tekno's head in, killing him, with a cry of "Back to work, dreamer!". The other miners are stunned, and they dash to gather around Tekno's dead body.

Minute 5

Drums suddenly start to play on the soundtrack, accompanied by backing vocals. In one powerful shot, a forced perspective from above, we hear a guard yelling at the miners to go back to work. Visually, the shot comes from the guard's point of

FIGURE 3 Neptune Frost *directed by Saul Williams and Anisia Uzeyman © Kino Lorber 2021. All rights reserved.*

view—which is to say his eyes—as he stands above the pit, looking down. All we see of the guard's own body is his hand, pointing impatiently as it enters and exits the frame. The miners themselves are at the bottom of the pit, huddled around Tekno's dead body. In this way, the shot literalizes the power relations of the mine. Eventually, the miners all return to work, except for Tekno's brother Matalusa (Bertrand Ninteretse aka "Kaya Free"), who continues to mourn as he holds the dead body. Matalusa and Tekno alike wear blue jumpsuits; the other miners are variously clad in bright colors. Neptune's voice-over continues; now she speaks of the ways that pain and suffering are transformed into money: "metal precious currency . . . heartbeat currency . . . that old black-bodied currency." Abstract value is derived from extorted physical labor. Addressing Western viewers directly, Neptune tells us that the cash value of the product is composed out of "all that you pay not to see." The camera pans across the mining pit, and up a rise on the far side. Here we see a crew of drummers, the source of the music (prior to this, we could not tell if the drumming, backed by singing, was diegetic or not). Williams and Uzeyman note in an interview that "the ensemble of Burundian drummers were in fact refugees," having fled to Rwanda to escape the civil war in their own country (Tham 2022). Recordings of this group, *Les Maitres-Tambours du Burundi*, are available in the West (Dwek 2021). Williams and Uzeyman note that these drum rhythms come from an old tradition, but they add that such rhythms have been cross-fertilized with recent developments in Western popular music, such as "electronic music, drum'n'bass and trap" (Tham 2022). Saul Williams' own musical compositions for *Neptune Frost* also display these influences. I am reminded of the slogan "ancient to the future," used by the Art Ensemble of Chicago for its "mix of musics—from the deeply spiritual to the fiercely experimental" (ECM Records 2018). In a similar way, the music in *Neptune Frost* expresses multiple temporalities all at once. This music is derived from ancient African traditions; it reflects contemporary social realities as well as contemporary musical developments; *and* beyond both of these, it projects toward a hoped-for later time of liberation. The futurity envisioned by *Neptune Frost* is something like what the Marxist philosopher Ernst Bloch called the *not-yet*. Bloch describes a possibility that is real in its own right, even though it is not for the moment actual: a potential for growth and change "which is not merely exhausted like an acorn in the enclosed realization of the oak-tree, but which has not yet ripened the whole of its internal and external conditions" (Bloch 1986/1959). The dense audiovisual layers of *Neptune Frost* convey a sense of time that is saturated and charged by such potentiality. The film is not limited to an immediate present; it loops back into the past and spills over toward an imminent but as-yet-unarrived future. In this way, *Neptune Frost* exemplifies Gilles Deleuze's claim that, in cinema, "the image is not in the present"; rather, "the image renders time relations—relations that can't be reduced to the present—sensible and visible" (interview in Flaxman 2000).

Minute 6

In the immediate aftermath of Tekno's murder, Matalusa struggles to drag his brother's body out of the pit. Meanwhile, all the other miners have been forced to return to work. They dig, they excavate, and they sort through the rocks that they have dislodged. The drumming and singing that accompany these efforts fit into the long tradition of *work songs* that help "to coordinate timing" among slaves or workers (Wikipedia 2024b). But *Neptune Frost* knowingly pushes this to a point of exaggeration and rupture. As the camera once again pans across the pit, the workers move in time with the drummers' rhythms: in effect, they are dancing. Some of the miners even mime the action of digging, pushing their picks back and forth, but without actually touching them to the ground. In a radical break with any sort of naturalist depiction, the film transforms their heavy labor into a sort of musical production number. As Uzeyman says in an interview, in shooting the film she was concerned with "how the camera moves with the choreography, and then how it incorporates the colors as meanings as well as a beat" (Gates 2022). This is the closest that the film comes to the massive dance numbers in Hollywood and Bollywood musical films. However, it is important to note that, although the miners' motions display powerful rhythms, these motions are not entirely coordinated with one another. That is to say, we are not given the large-scale patterns of bodies in perfect synchronization that we find in more traditional musicals. Busby Berkeley's extravagant production numbers in Hollywood films of the 1930s are often interpreted as reflecting the organization of factories of the time, with their Fordist assembly lines and Taylorist time management (e.g., Doane 2002). By contrast, the motions of the miners in *Neptune Frost* are not so rigidly coordinated with one another. There is a certain looseness here; we might say that the armed guards are needed in the mine precisely because its labor process cannot quite be rationalized in the manner of a Fordist factory. In any case, the dancing does not mitigate the horror of Tekno's murder. Nonetheless, the miners' dance still offers a premonition of the potential utopian transfiguration of their labor. The drumming is crucial because of how it opposes the standardization and uniformity of twentieth-century commodity production. Rather, this drumming exemplifies the way that syncopated rhythms play such a great role in twentieth- and twenty-first-century popular music. As Mark Abel argues, syncopation "generate[s] flexibility and unpredictability." It breaks up "the highly measured temporality of the contemporary world." More specifically, syncopation undermines the hegemony of homogeneous clock time, which rules over the industrial capitalist labor process. In opposition to such optimized and mechanistically ordered time, the "dislocated instances" of beats in syncopation, "having shattered time's essential flow, are woven into a new temporal continuum" (Abel 2014). In the drumming here, as in its other uses of music, song, and dance, *Neptune Frost* pushes toward a reconfigured, ecstatic temporality: an experience of time beyond the reach of capitalist work discipline.

Minute 7

The dancing and the drumming continue; the drummers are now in the pit alongside the miners, rather than perching above it. Matalusa gets a firm grip on Tekno's body and finally succeeds in lifting it out of the pit. The camera pulls back, and the title NEPTUNE FROST finally appears on the screen, written in two highly stylized fonts (one for each word). Over the title, we hear the same electronic motif that we heard in the very first minute of the movie. Finally, as Matalusa carries Tekno's body away, the drumming cuts out, and the film cuts back to Neptune's story. We will not see Matalusa again until he has already arrived in Digitaria. Williams says in an interview that the (unreleased) graphic novel version of the story focuses on Matalusa's journey to the refuge, while the movie instead gives us Neptune's journey (Keogan 2022). We see Neptune, still male, sitting alone in his house, and braiding his hair. It is nighttime, and the room is barely lit. This is the first of a number of sequences in the film that are largely dark. We have a hard time picking out faces and figures; but this is also what allows, as Jourdain Searles puts it, for "Black skin" to be "lovingly shot, glowing with purple and blue light" (Searles 2021). Uzeyman notes that, here and throughout the film, she uses "low key lighting," combined with "colorful bounces, reflectors, diffuser grid and a great deal of gels" in order "to create moody contrasts and brilliance with a mythical feel" (Filmmaker Staff 2022). In any case, at the same time that light is diffused and scattered in these sequences, or even reduced to minimal levels, the movie's sound remains crisp. As Neptune works on his hair, there is a knock on the door. Neptune turns his head as he hears the noise. There is a slight, barely noticeable, jump cut here, since the next shot shows Neptune already standing and holding a lantern as he opens the door. The pastor who presided over the funeral comes into the house.

Minute 8

The pastor enters Neptune's hut, still spouting religious bromides as he did before. Neptune barely responds, with a mumbled "Thank you, Pastor" and "Yes, Pastor." The screen is still extremely dark, and things are difficult to see. Neptune places the lantern on a table. The pastor sits on a bench next to the table, and pats the bench, inviting Neptune to sit next to him, on the other side from the lamp. Their faces and upper bodies, lit by the lantern, glimmer out of the darkness, like in a painting by Caravaggio, only with Black people instead of white. In extreme close-up, we see Neptune turn his face away from the pastor who is looking toward him and addressing him. As the pastor continues to deliver his canned phrases of comfort, he puts his arm around Neptune, and pulls him close in an unwanted embrace. The pastor seems to be leaning in to Neptune for a kiss. This abuse may lead us to recall news reports that sexual abuse by priests has apparently been widespread throughout the second half of the twentieth century and well into the twenty-first century (Graham 2023).

Minute 9

The screen is still extremely dark. Resisting the pastor's abuse, Neptune violently pushes him away and knocks him down. After a moment of uncertainty, Neptune gets up. He quickly stuffs a few items into a bag, most notably a red dress, which is only on screen for a moment, but which will be important later, when Neptune in female aspect wears it. Neptune puts on a jacket and leaves the house. Now there's a cut to an entirely different scene. It is still nighttime, but we are back at the coltan mine. We see dim, blurry shots of the miners at work in the dark. They are lit only by a reddish glow that casts shadows and that is most distinct on the wall of the pit behind them. Perhaps this is the moonlight? Since we can barely see anything, the most prominent feature of this part of the film is the music on the soundtrack. A chorus of male voices is chanting: "These MotherFuckers Don't Want To Back Down." The miners do not seem to be the ones singing, even though their work motions are still rhythmic as they were before. Where does the chanting come from, then? This is a common procedure throughout the film: a motif, is introduced, whose source and context will only become apparent later. *Neptune Frost* continually weaves together a variety of elements in this manner, creating a promiscuous mixture of sights and sounds— or better, a dense audiovisual polyphonic and polyrhythmic assemblage.

Minute 10

The sound of the chant fades out and is replaced by birds chirping as the film cuts from the mine to a horizontal camera movement that shows the forest just before dawn, with an orange glow from the not-yet-risen Sun visible beyond the trees. Neptune gathers water from an open pipe and then walks past piles of yellow plastic shipping containers. This reminds us that there are always close connections between the rural African locations in which the movie takes place and the metropoles of the world economy (which are mostly located in North America, Western Europe, and East Asia). The former provide the raw materials that are used in the latter for the manufacture of digital devices. Once these devices have been sold and used, and have broken down, worn out, or been replaced by upgrades, their debris are sent back to Africa as e-waste. As Neptune walks, he sings to himself the same chant we have already heard: "These MotherFuckers Don't Want To Back Down." We still have no context for this song; we don't yet know who sang it first or where and when Neptune might have heard it. It might well be most accurate to say that Neptune heard it on the movie's soundtrack, just as we did. This is not a metacinematic gesture, however, but rather a suggestion that there are no meta-levels at all. The world system, which the movie both depicts and belongs to, is a sphere of radical immanence, alike in economic, social, and material terms. The movie therefore makes immediate connections, thanks to the powers of editing, between ostensibly distant and mutually distinct realms. This is a necessary precondition for any effort (by characters within the movie, as well as by the movie itself) first to grasp the world system and then to endeavor to escape it and to subvert it. What we have here, then, is neither classical Eisensteinian montage, which claims to show us the dialectical unity of clashing opposites, nor Hollywood continuity montage, which claims to create a stable unity of time, space, and causality. Rather, montage in *Neptune Frost* displays a fluid accretion of associations; this mirrors the way that, in Eisenstein's later work, according to Joan Neuberger, montage no longer just enacts the battle of opposites, but also provides a way that disparate elements can "merge into, or interpenetrate, one another" (Neuberger 2019). This makes for an aesthetic of accretion and connection. Saul Williams tells us, in his Director's Statement, that "the connection was there before the machine" and that "*Neptune Frost* is a story that demystifies the connection. . . . Maybe it unlocks something" (Kino Lorber 2022). The West, as those of us who live within it today know it and take it for granted, could not exist without Africa. The "machine" of trade, manufacture, and digital networks cuts across all these distances. This is all the more so in that the West systematically ignores its ties to Africa and conceals its reliance upon Africa. Neptune passes by a village; a left-to-right tracking shot from his own point of view shows us what is very nearly a tableau vivant of the town's central square. There are people both standing and seated; they barely move as they look straight ahead toward the camera, which is to say toward Neptune. There are also a few bicycles and some animals resting on the ground. The next shot, seemingly continuous with this one, is formally a reverse shot; Neptune pauses and glances toward screen left, suggesting that he is looking back at the village square that he has just walked by. However, this shot plays in reverse motion: the only shot in the entire movie to do so. Behind Neptune, children at play run backward; an adult woman, entering the frame at the left, also seems to walk backward. We hear the call of a bird, apparently coming from offscreen right. The bird's cry unfolds forward in time, if we can judge by the attack and decay of the sound, even though the images are playing backward. In any case, Neptune turns his head from left to right, seeming to shift his attention toward the source of the sound (at the very least, this would be the correct description if the shot were running forward in time). There is a cut to a distant shot of a bird flying, forward in time, through the cloudy sky.

Minute 11

Another cut, and the camera moves downward from the trees and toward the ground. Yet another quick cut takes us to an entirely new scene, in a new location. We see a student protest, probably taking place in the nation's capitol. A mass of students, mostly male, are marching, holding signs, banging drums, waving fists in the air, and chanting at full volume the phrase we have previously heard: "These MotherFuckers Don't Want To Back Down." Now we finally know this chant's diegetic source. Many of the students, but not all, wear white shirts with ties (presumably their school uniform) and also carry yellow backpacks. These colors contrast with the bright pink shirts worn by the police, who also wear mesh masks over their faces. The camera is placed behind the backs of the policemen. First we see the student protesters moving away, but then the camera position is shifted, so that we are just behind the policemen as they form a line in order to hold back the students who are trying to push forward. The camera tracks from left to right, behind the policemen, as they hold a line against the mass of protesters. The movie will not develop the story of the student protesters further, except for a few flashbacks when one of the protesters comes to Digitaria and recounts his experiences. But the film works by accumulating these other scenes, or points of reference, that give us additional context for the actions of Neptune and Matalusa and for the status of Digitaria. In any case, the next cut returns us to Neptune in the village. The sound of the student chant continues across the cut. But now we hear the chant in a tinny tone and at a much lower volume; it is being broadcast from small plastic hexagonal wireless devices, which several children hold up and avidly watch as they walk along. The revolutionary chant is broadcast everywhere. We cut from this to silence and to close-ups of Neptune walking—first we see him from behind and then from in front, with his face almost filling the screen. As Neptune continues to walk, he takes out and scrutinizes the same sort of hexagonal electronic device that the children were carrying earlier. He resumes singing the chant. Neptune arrives at what seems to be another village; for a moment, the chant reverts to its tinny lower-volume broadcast version. In a striking long shot and then a somewhat closer one, Neptune again sings the chant as he walks in between buildings draped with sheets that are wrapped around their frames in place of walls. The film is rich in closely perceived details; but it also emphasizes the fact that, throughout our world, and as much in Africa as in the West, all that is solid melts into air.

Minute 12

Another brief transitional shot gives us, once again, the call and the sight of a bird soaring through the air. Neptune walks toward the camera and passes through a narrow rectangular aperture right in the center of the frame, in the gap between two enormous tree trunks that darken the sides of the image. As Neptune passes through, we get a tight reverse shot with the tree trunks close to the camera and Neptune behind them, having barely fit through the gap. He looks upward. Though the shots can be understood entirely naturalistically, they are also composed in such a way as to suggest the passage through a portal and into another (magical?) world. Suddenly, it is dark again. We can barely see Neptune standing by the trunk of a gigantic tree. The film cuts from this to a shot of the moon, nearly full, suspended in the dark sky. A voice starts whispering, and a new melody starts playing. Neptune is asleep at the base of the tree. The whisper amplifies into a speaking voice. A man looms over Neptune's sleeping form. This is the Wheel Man, as he will later be called by Matalusa—though he is listed in the credits as "Potolo the Avatar" (Eric Ngangare "1Key"). The Wheel Man has big white balls of matted hair hanging down over both sides of his face. And he wears a sort of headdress, with spokes from which four slowly revolving bicycle wheels are extended. Williams says in an interview that "Potolo comes from the Dogon [people of West Africa] and means [the star] Sirius"; but he adds that this different location is not irrelevant to Rwanda and Burundi, since Potolo enunciates "ancient mythologies that cross the [African] continent." Even as the film is tightly focused on one location, it also extends out to reference pan-African longings, as well as the role of coltan mining in Congo-Rwanda-Burundi within the economic world system. The extension is both spatial and temporal. Long before the invention of modern technologies, Williams reminds us, the drum in Africa was "the first form of wireless communication" (Burton 2022). As before with the drumming, so here as well with the transmission from the Wheel Man, the film works with a wide range of eclectic, transverse, and syncretic procedures. It thereby constructs a prospect of liberation out of whatever materials are at hand, old or new. Such an aesthetic practice, ancient and yet never obsolete, is what Claude Lévi-Strauss calls *bricolage*: the art of "mak[ing] do with 'whatever is at hand'—that is to say, a set of tolls and materials that is finite at each moment, as well as heterogeneous, because the composition of the set . . . is the contingent result of all the occasions that have presented themselves" over a series of experiences (Lévi-Strauss 2021; see also Derrida 1978).

Minute 13

If the Wheel Man is a *bricoleur*, he is also a kind of reality hacker (Wikipedia 2024c). He urges his listeners to *hack*, not just into computers but also into everything else: "land rights and ownership . . . business law, proprietorship . . . the history of the bank . . . the business of slavery [and] free labor . . . into ambition and greed, into suffering and sufferance." This litany encompasses the long history of Africa's interactions with, and exploitation by, powers from other parts of the

FIGURE 4 Neptune Frost *directed by Saul Williams and Anisia Uzeyman © Kino Lorber 2021. All rights reserved.*

world. The kidnapping and enslavement of Africans on a vast scale was the motor behind the rise of capitalism in the West, even as capitalism went on to replace formal slavery with the exploitation of so-called "free labor." The Wheel Man asks us to explore this history and to undo it. Though his speech is continuous and uninterrupted, an editing cut gives us a change of location. We are now indoors, in a dim room lit only by banks of computer monitors, which all display a bluish tinge. The Wheel Man is no longer addressing the slumbering Neptune, but rather a young man and a young woman, both of whom are awake and listen to him avidly. They seem to be dream avatars of Neptune (female) and of Matalusa. They both wear white shirts like the protesting students, and they both have semicircles of tiny neon lights embedded in their foreheads—a fashion that will become more prominent later in the film when we see it in Digitaria. The continuous vocal and instrumental sound, and the uniformity of bluish lighting, work to make the sequence feel continuous despite the shift from a real location to an apparently phantasmatic one. This formal approach is an inversion of what goes on in many art films of the later twentieth century. For instance, French New Wave directors like Jean-Luc Godard often seek to disrupt the viewing experience and make us more aware of the constructed nature of cinematic representation by violating expected formal conventions as ostentatiously as possible. Edits like jump cuts, or like a shot in which a character moves across the screen from left to right, followed by one in which the same character, continuing the same action, now moves instead from right to left, work to make us aware of how even seemingly naturalistic details in the film are in fact governed by preexisting formal rules. By contrast, *Neptune Frost* gathers together disparate scenes and disparate phenomena, and uses visual and sonic continuities to conflate them, and make them seem cohesive with one another. This is *bricolage* in action. It does not feel like anything has changed, except for a widening of range, when the Wheel Man addresses both Neptune and Matalusa in a dream vision that they both seem to share. He starts singing instead of talking, along with the same melody that is already playing on the soundtrack. His words move from the pragmatics of hacking into a mythical register: "once upon a time, very long ago."

Minute 14

The sequence with the Wheel Man continues. He sings about how "my mother and father were binary stars," referring to the Dogon understanding of the binary star Sirius. He also mentions "binary crime theory"; this striking phrase is not directly explained, but perhaps it refers to the binary logic of Western thought with regard to gender and other matters: a logic that *Neptune Frost* is concerned to take apart. Williams speaks explicitly in an interview about how "gender fluidity ... is the breaking of the binary" (Obenson 2021). The Wheel Man sings of the creation of the world and of the first appearance of day and light. This is a polyglot discourse, as the Wheel Man continually switches between English, French, and African languages. The Wheel Man reaches out his hands to the young man and the young woman and addresses them directly. As they listen to him, they look back and forth at one another. And, of course, the Wheel Man's lesson is also being addressed to us, the viewers. I feel a sense of wonder at the magical density of this scene, as well as at the way that the future and the past join hands so that computers meld seamlessly with traditional practices. The action is barely visible; the Wheel Man's words are enigmatic; Neptune and Matalusa have not met yet in real life; and the music is lulling in its repetitions. And yet the scene is both absorbing and momentous, in a way that I cannot easily describe in words. This scene is more than just images and sounds. I am absorbed in a wondrous sense of "*synaesthesia* and *coenaesthesia*"—to cite the peak forms of embodied "cross-modal" perception described by Vivian Sobchack in her beautiful and compelling account of cinematic experience (Sobchack 2004).

Minute 15

The Wheel Man continues speaking and singing in a mythical register: "And then there was fire." Neptune and Matalusa join him in the chorus of his song: "fire in the sky, fire in the sky," repeated a number of times. The Wheel Man's visionary account raises the possibility of apocalyptic change, even though this change remains latent and does not actually take place. In any case, now we seem to be out of doors again, rather than in the computer room of a few moments before. We catch a quick glimpse of the moon, shining through a halo of clouds. The Wheel Man gyrates back and forth, his head filling the dark screen in a sort of dance. The bicycle wheels in his headdress spin slowly and majestically. The moonlight illuminates the white shirts worn by the young people, and there seems to be motion, barely perceptible, at the edge of the frame. This scene conveys a powerful sense of mystery and also of a respite from the threats and the stresses that have filled the movie up to this point: the sexual abuse of Neptune by the pastor; the harsh, murderous discipline of the coltan pit; the police confrontation with the students. The Wheel Man is a singular presence; after this scene, he will not reappear in the film, except when he is remembered by Matalusa in a brief flashback. But his emphasis upon the practice of hacking, and his call for rebellion, haunt the remainder of the film. With this scene's reach through the vastnesses of space and time, and its indeterminate location, we may once again recall Deleuze's maxim that "it is not quite right to say that the cinematographic image is in the present." Rather, the image is "a set of relationships of time," with past and future dimensions that generate our sense of the present, but also extend well beyond it (Deleuze 1989). To compress this into a formula, we may say, after Deleuze, that cinema "evades the present" (Deleuze 1990).

Minute 16

The Wheel Man's song continues for another half minute. Through the dark, we briefly glimpse an array of electric lights on or near the ground, but the camera moves upward to give us another sight of the moon. The nighttime scene with the moon slowly fades out; it is replaced by a long shot of the landscape in the daytime, with a big tree and cloudy skies. The music of the Wheel Man's song also fades out. Neptune, in male form, is still asleep under the tree. Although the scene with the Wheel Man is presented as a dream vision, it is audiovisually impressive enough, and emotionally compelling enough, that we cannot dismiss it as being merely phantasmatic or subjective. The nocturnal realm of the Wheel Man is a new dimension—one of considerable weight—in the world of the film. There are many realms of being, and they affect one another in unexpected ways. Now that it is daytime,

Neptune wakes up and stretches into a sitting position. He is under the same tree as when he went to sleep; he has not physically moved, even if he traversed an entirely different realm in his dream vision. Neptune reaches into his pack for some food, which he starts to eat, still sitting under the tree. Though very little actually happens during this minute of the film, it effectively conveys the transition from sleep to waking: which is to say, in the terms that the film suggests to us, from one ontological realm to another.

Minute 17

As Neptune sits and eats, there is a cut to a shot of the tree's leaves and branches above him, from his own point of view. At the same moment, the female Neptune's voice-over returns on the soundtrack: "A story always has a beginning, just as each has many interpretations, like dreams." The film cuts back to a shot of the male Neptune under the tree, but closer up than before. This small sequence (shot-reverse shot plus voice-over) beautifully encapsulates the movie's overall argument. We are aligned with a particular point of view—as opposed to some ideal of universality and objectivity. But this point of view, in its very specificity, is itself also divided, since it is both male and female. Singularity ("a beginning") overlaps with multiplicity ("many interpretations"). After this, the male Neptune starts singing, but a different song than before: "Everyone knows when the sunrise / See it dawn in their own eye [*sic*]." The song's lyrics further emphasize the same argument: the sunrise is universal, but everyone experiences it in their own particular way. As Neptune's singing continues, the film cuts to a shot of him walking away from the camera, away from the same portal between two trees that he approached and entered in Minute 12. This closes a sort of parenthesis in the film; we return from the visionary realm to that of the everyday. Next, we see shots of Neptune continuing to sing as he walks through a field. The camera tracks with him as he moves screen right to screen left. The chorus of his song states that there is "no turning back." Neptune is definitively committed to his voyage of transformation. A woman with a baby tied to her back looks back at him with curiosity after crossing his path. Or perhaps she is looking back at the camera, surprised to find herself in a movie. As I have already maintained, there are no meta-levels in this movie, so it is impossible to decide between these two interpretations. In any case, it would seem that Neptune stands out, apart from the world in which he has lived up until now.

Minute 18

The same sequence continues, but now Neptune, followed by a tracking shot, is walking screen left to screen right. He arrives at a wide road and turns away from the camera to walk down it. An ominous repeating motif plays on the soundtrack. Now Neptune is in a town, bigger and more populous than the village he walked past before. Neptune looks around uncertainly, or in surprise—perhaps because he has never been in a town of such size before. People on bicycles, mopeds, and even a truck pass him by. We see this traffic and hear the motors of the mopeds on the soundtrack. But nobody pays attention to Neptune or interacts with him in any way. The film continues to alternate between shots of Neptune walking in different screen directions. He slowly whirls around in apparent confusion, and then starts jogging for a few seconds, in what looks like slow motion. Finally he walks toward the camera, past a wall painted bluish-green.

Minute 19

The same ominous musical motif continues, but we also hear the sound of waves of water. Neptune has come to a large lake.

He gets into a boat with about a dozen passengers in order to pass across the lake. The repeated musical motif finally fades out. A close shot of Neptune's face, framed by reeds growing on the shore of the lake behind him, gives way to a longer shot of the boat turning and heading into open water. The sky is somewhat cloudy, but the water is peaceful. The boat moves away from the camera in a long shot. We glimpse the far shore, with hills, in the distance. A close-up of Neptune sitting in the boat gives way to a close-up of a young woman sitting opposite, wearing a red scarf over a yellow dress. She is not looking back toward Neptune but rather in an entirely different direction, out toward the water. So although the film returns to the close shot of Neptune, this is not quite the shot/reverse shot reciprocal structure that we have seen previously and that we take for granted in mainstream narrative films. Rather, things remain open. There is no reciprocity here, but also no hostility. All of the passengers are caught in their own private thoughts, minding their own business. The boat takes us, just as it takes Neptune, away from any certainty or closure.

Minute 20

There is no dialogue, and no non-diegetic music, during this minute. All we can hear is the low sound of the boat's engine as it progresses through the water. The camera remains close to Neptune, moving up and down his body. He is sitting next to a woman holding a baby. He grabs the baby's hand for a moment, but the baby immediately pulls away from him and returns its attention to its mother. This reinforces our sense of Neptune's isolation. But perhaps such loneliness also gives him a certain degree of freedom. Neptune takes a pair of women's high-heeled shoes out of his bag and carefully puts them on. They just barely fit, and he must take care and effort to get his feet solidly within them. We cut to a further-away shot, still with Neptune in the foreground, but wide enough to show the other passengers on the boat. Neptune looks around warily; he seems to be checking to make sure that none of the others have noticed his shoes. The woman in the yellow dress smiles slightly, though we cannot tell whether or not this is in response to Neptune's action.

Minute 21

We return to a much closer shot of Neptune, as he picks up his bag, opens it, and once again fusses with its contents. The ominous repeated musical phrase fades in. This time, Neptune takes the red dress out of his bag. He holds the dress to his face and sniffs it avidly. From one shot to the next, as he looks upward after sniffing the dress, the sky has become dark. As Neptune looks upward, the electric lights on the edge of the pergola that partly shields the boat from the sky have turned on. Now it is night. A second repeated musical motif, played on a trumpet, joins the previous one. This second motif is less ominous and more anticipatory in tone. Over a series of shots, Neptune continues to look and to reach upward. In a much longer shot, we see the boat arriving at its destination and the passengers disembarking in the dark. Neptune walks away from the dock and toward a spot where a group of children are singing, dancing, and jumping up and down. It is nighttime, and the children cannot be seen very clearly, but their shadows are silhouetted against a lit-up white wall.

Minute 22

This minute contains the beginning of an important inflection point in the course of the film: Neptune's change of gender. As Neptune passes by the children, he joins them for a moment, jumping up and down with them; we see this in a long shot. Then Neptune walks on. But now the film becomes nearly abstract, in a dense audiovisual way. We hear the sound of a motorcycle or moped; then we see a close-up of Neptune's backlit profile. We hear the sounds of a crash. There are rapid cuts and shots with circles of light in an otherwise entirely dark frame. We cannot quite make out what has happened, but our best guess is that the crashing sounds mean that Neptune has been knocked down by the passing vehicle. Several shots looking up from the ground show the children leaning over Neptune, with concern marked on their faces. The camera wobbles, and the childrens' faces go in and out of focus. Shots of the children are intercut with more shots of circles of light against a background darkness. At this point, we seem to have a subjective camera: its shakings and unfocusings give us a sense of Neptune's injured and confused state. Electronic squawks on the soundtrack contribute to the overall sense of disorientation. A woman, Binya (Natacha Muziramakenga), comes up and helps Neptune get back on his feet.

Minute 23

The same electronic fragments keep playing, over and over. Binya helps Neptune hobble away. We see their profiles from behind, with a wobbly handheld camera following them; this perspective is intercut with close-ups of the left side of Neptune's face, from Binya's point of view. Now we are indoors, in a room. Neptune has been seated. It is still mostly dark, with first reddish and then bluish accents on the wall behind Neptune and Binya. Neptune tries to speak, but he feels weak and collapses; Binya cradles his head and lays him down gently on the floor. Binya speaks enigmatically to Neptune: "The Motherboard is bleeding. . . . This is the moment . . . Unanimous goldmine. . . . The power of the subconscious is honed through guidance." These are phrases that we will hear again later on in the film. The Motherboard "is the main printed circuit board (PCB) in general-purpose computers and other expandable systems. It holds and allows communication between many of the crucial electronic components of a system" (Wikipedia 2024e). Later on, in Digitaria, Neptune in her female aspect will be identified as the Motherboard. "Unanimous goldmine" is also a phrase that we will hear repeated throughout the film; it is the common greeting of the hackers in Digitaria. Binya is the second prophetic voice we hear in the movie, after the Wheel Man. She aids Neptune in her metamorphosis and foretells the crucial role she will play in contesting the power of the worldwide network.

Minute 24

Binya continues to fuss over Neptune, leaning over him and trying to make him comfortable. She also continues to speak prophetically, urging Neptune to "sense the connection. . . . What birth has severed, love will reconnect." There is a shot/reverse shot setup between Neptune lying prone on the floor and Binya, with her wild locks, hovering over him. Neptune is wearing a white shirt, so that the shots showing him are somewhat brighter than those showing Binya. At a certain point, Binya breaks into song, just as the Wheel Man did earlier. This is another scene of commentary, a bit like that provided by the Chorus in ancient drama. As Binya sings, the wavering camera movements over Neptune's body are intercut with outdoor shots of the landscape at night. The moon is visible, low in the sky, seen through a scrim of trees. Extreme close-ups of Neptune's face alternate with slightly more distanced close-ups of Binya's face, together with shots of a bird with white head and reddish neck, seen in profile facing toward screen left. The bird is out of focus at first, but soon it resolves and can be seen clearly. It caws and trills. This bird will reappear throughout the film; we will eventually learn that its name is Frost, thereby giving us the other half of the movie's title. Throughout these shots, Binya continues to sing; her lyrics speak of her doubt and despair, as well as of "light years," indicating the vastness of the universe. But the song also contains an inspirational message for Neptune: an exhortation for him/her to "picture a dream and dare to live it / Open your soul and dare to give it."

Minute 25

Binya continues singing; all the lyrics are repeated. The lighting remains dim. The screen is quite dark, though sometimes reddish tonalities, and other times bluish tonalities, stand out from the murk. The camera moves slowly in nearly every shot, exploring a limited area—a face, a small patch of the floor—even though it is too dark to make out anything distinctly. The distribution of shots remains similar to that of the previous minute. But there is also interpolated shots of a woman, with shaved head, holding the bird, followed by blurry extreme close-ups of the bird's body and the woman's upper face. Since the lighting of these shots matches closely with that of all the other shots, it does not register as disjunctive. But we have not seen this particular character before. And when we see her again, it will be with entirely different lighting and in an entirely different location. The woman is Memory (Eliane Umuhire), whom we will later encounter at much greater length in the hacker enclave of Digitaria. There, Memory is—among other things—the bird's caretaker. This is another example of the post-Eisensteinian accretive montage, already mentioned in my comments on Minute 10. *Neptune Frost* often gives us images and sounds we have not encountered before and only provides a context subsequently. This is one important reason for the mysterious feeling of *density* that is produced when I watch this film. Williams and Uzeyman repeatedly make use of figural, associative juxtapositions: matching different characters and different locations in a manner that is not reducible to the demands of the narrative. Rather, *Neptune Frost* uses such visual juxtapositions in order to produce multidimensional resonances, connecting various characters and feelings across disparate space-time coordinates.

Minute 26

The song continues, and the same style of montage continues. The film in general works this way: it establishes sequences with a unified atmosphere, even as it absorbs incongruities. As we watch and listen, we move from one homogeneous zone to another. In the course of this minute, we encounter a few more odd details. For instance, the room in which Neptune is lying has playing cards strewn all over the floor; though we glimpsed this briefly before, now it becomes a focus of our attention in its own right. Now the camera movement is more fluid than it was during the previous minutes in Binya's shack. The camera spins in a fluid half-circle around the floor, with its playing cards scattered everywhere. We may say that, at this point, the film renders for us a *tactile space*, to use (or abuse) a concept from Deleuze. This happens when "space itself has left behind its own co-ordinates and its metric relations." Space is no longer a preexisting matrix that defines a fixed volume. Instead, this space is only actualized to the extent that the camera moves through it. Deleuze uses the concept in his discussion of how the camera matches the exploratory movements of hands and feet in Robert Bresson's films (Deleuze 1986). In *Neptune Frost*, the technique is not bound to the body in this way; but—as we will discover in the next minute—it is still used in order to express a process of bodily metamorphosis. At the same time that the camera stays with the floor in this exacting way, Binya sings about "people beyond the moon." We have, therefore, a juxtaposition of near and far: of space as it is immediately moved through on the one hand, and of space as an inconceivably vast extent, far beyond corporeal reach, on the other. In the course of this sequence, we also get one more shot of Memory sitting quietly in the darkness as the bird flies off from her hand and into the open air. This is followed, as before, by two extreme close-ups: first of the bird's pinkish body and second of the upper portion of Memory's face, with the screen filled by her nose, her open eyes, and her forehead. The close-up of Memory's face is clearer and lasts slightly longer, than was the case in the previous minute; we clearly see the broken transistor that is pasted onto her forehead as a piece of jewelry. We will see much more of this style when we get to Digitaria. But at this point in the film, we only have the darkness that we associate with the room into which Binya took Neptune. Binya repeats the same line of the song, about the moon, over and over. But finally, toward the end of the minute, Binya speaks, rather than sings, a final line: "This is what happens next."

Minute 27

The film is galvanized by Binya's singing, as we wait for the extraordinary event that indeed happens next. There is another

FIGURE 5 Neptune Frost *directed by Saul Williams and Anisia Uzeyman* © *Kino Lorber 2021. All rights reserved.*

cut to Neptune lying on the floor, even as the singer enunciates a final word: "breath." But now Neptune is suddenly female. Cheryl Isheja replaces Elvis Ngabo aka "Bobo" in the role. She looks up at the camera, opening her eyes wide and smiling. She is now wearing the red dress that the male Neptune fussed over before. There are tiny neon lights embedded in the rims of Neptune's eyes, similar to those on the young people's foreheads when the Wheel Man was singing to them. The film cuts to a long shot of trees and sky, with silence on the soundtrack; the night is finally over, and it is getting light. Then we cut back to a shot of Neptune getting up from off the ground. Her posture, lying on her back, is the same as in the previous shot, and the camera hovers over her face just as it did before. But we can now see that Neptune is outdoors, lying on a large flat rock overlooking greenery, instead of on the floor of Binya's house. This is followed by long shots of the female Neptune walking through the landscape, just as the male Neptune did before. Neptune's voice-over addresses the confusion that we might well be feeling at this point: "Maybe you're asking yourself WTF is this? Is it a poet's idea of a dream?" A moment later, her voice-over tells us that "what blossomed as understanding had been planted in years of confusion." This presumably refers to the long span of years, already mentioned in Minute 2, between Neptune's physical birth and her awakening as female now, in her twenty-third year. Williams recounts, in an interview, that he was worried about how the mother of Kaya (the actor playing Matalusa) might react to the gender transition at the center of the film, since she was "very religious." But when told the plot of the film, Kaya's mother said: "Oh, that old story, that's a Burundian folk tale. Kaya, don't you remember, we've always told this story. This is an old story" (Ngema 2022; cf. also Gates 2022). We Western viewers need to abandon our all-too-common presuppositions either that gender and sexuality are understood throughout the world in the same way as they are in our own societies, or else that other parts of the world have more "backward" values in this regard than "we" do. In any case, as the now-female Neptune walks along, she sings out loud the same song about the sunrise that the male Neptune was singing during Minute 17.

Minute 28

This is a minute of transitions. The now-female Neptune continues singing the same song, standing still and looking up at the sky, before she resumes walking away from the camera. As her singing continues, the camera abandons her and tilts upward, showing us the vast green landscape extending beyond her and then cutting to other long shots of landscape, more blue than green because they show more of the sky. Neptune's singing voice fades out. The landscape fades out and another shot fades in: we are in the air, over the blurry tops of the trees, while the bird's head and upper body, extremely close by, enter from frame right. From here, we cut to a shot from above, looking down at some trees. The bird makes another entrance, again from frame right. In this way, we leave Neptune to her wanderings and move to an entirely different location, with other characters.

Minute 29

We are now, finally, in the hacker refuge of Digitaria, where most of the rest of the film will take place. The name evidently references digital technologies. But *Digitaria* is also the scientific name for the plant that the Dogon people of West Africa call *po*; this plant, in turn, gives its name to *Potolo*, the designation in Dogon mythology for the star that astronomers now call Sirius B, the smaller binary companion of Sirius. We have already met the Wheel Man, who is named Potolo. Once again, although *Neptune Frost* is specifically rooted in Rwanda and Burundi, Williams and Uzeyman provide an additional layer of pan-African syncretism. In Digitaria, we encounter

FIGURE 6 Neptune Frost *directed by Saul Williams and Anisia Uzeyman* © *Kino Lorber 2021. All rights reserved.*

Elohel (Rebecca Muciyo), a woman wearing a red shirt and tan pants, with a cybernetic right arm and hand. The hand is black and multi-jointed; the arm from the elbow down is yellow and festooned with batteries and other small electronic devices. Elohel is already a cyborg, a human-machine hybrid. (We will learn later what happened to her original arm.) Elohel sits on a crate and smokes a cigarette. She is talking with Memory, whom we glimpsed in Minutes 25 and 26 but who is now presented to us in context for the first time. These characters' names are allegorically significant. Elohel sounds to me like a biblical prophet (think of Elijah and Elisha), but her name is also homonymous with the online expression "LOL." Memory is as deep and empathetic as her name implies. But she also turns out to be as limited as one might fear: for, although the faculty of memory is indispensable, it cannot do everything by itself. At the very least, it needs to be supplemented by imagination and will. As for the location in which we find ourselves, Digitaria is an e-waste dump. Large numbers of broken computer parts, including circuit boards, transistors, and screens, are strewn along the ground. In some places, they have been combined into assemblage-sculptures. This is one way that the African landscape of *Neptune Frost* is connected to the wider world. The West first extracts natural resources, such as coltan, from Africa in order to build phones and computers. But these devices only have a limited lifespan (planned obsolescence). At the other end of the cycle, the West sends its digital refuse back to Africa for disposal. As Williams describes it, "planes fly in e-waste from the Western world—old computers, phones, towers, hard drives, all of this stuff—and dump it in a place where scavenger culture is still alive, because there's copper and all of these things that can be recycled or reused" (Keogan 2022). In fact, he adds, "these e-waste camps across the continent and the world, are positioned near the mines where the coltan, cobalt, and all of the materials that go into our machinery are sourced" (Lucier 2024). Materials move from Africa to the West and then back again to Africa: it is an entire cycle of technological transformations. All this is reflected in Digitaria. Elohel and Memory—and the other inhabitants, whom we will meet later—adorn themselves with transistors and other "recycled computer parts" (Keogan 2022), which they wear as jewelry, in their ears, above their eyes, and affixed to their foreheads. This unusual look might be vividly, and even accurately, described as "cyberpunk"; but it is quite different from the look and feel of Western cyberpunk as it is expressed in novels, movies, and games. This unique fashion look, made from repurposed high-tech trash, was devised for the film by the Rwandan artist Cedric Mizero, serving here as costume designer, with assistance from hair and makeup director Tanya Melendez. In Uzeyman's words, "recycling material is also very hip-hop. It's very close to what nourishes us in terms of posture, and how you reclaim your own status and place and power" (Keogan 2022). The people of Digitaria turn their talents to subversive use. Elohel tells Memory how she works on sound systems and how a vision—"I dreamt and saw a wheel like Ezekiel"—drew her to come to this location deep in the forest. In response, Memory speaks of fleeing from the war, which "forced us into other dimensions, where the worst had already happened." Memory is especially able to commune with animals. In addition to all the other forms of adornment, she wears a bird's nest on her right shoulder. She tells Elohel that "birds are living witness. . . . They fly through portals where pain is the only passport." A moment later, we hear the call of the bird that we have encountered before. The next shot shows it, as usual, on the right edge of the frame. Memory calls to the bird, and it flies down in a blur of overlapping fuzzy shots and lands on her hand.

Minute 30

Matalusa appears, still wearing the blue jumpsuit he wore in the mine and walks toward Elohel and Memory. He is the third person, after the two of them, to have arrived in this forest refuge. He returns the women's greeting by saying "unanimous goldmine." The bird flies off Memory's shoulder, back into the trees. Matalusa complains of bad dreams; a lot of things are still unresolved. Elohel offers him a beer; he accepts, even though it is not chilled. Elohel explains that she hasn't yet figured out how to get electrical power here. As the camera pans down a tree trunk within which computer components seem to be embedded, Matalusa asks the obvious question: "what is this place?" Elohel and Memory tell him that it is "like another dimension . . . we choose dimensions like cities to live in." They also warn Matalusa that "man don't choose; woman choose [sic]." It is important to parse these claims carefully. Our actual world is shaped by computing and communications technologies; this is as true for people in the African forest as it is for me in a North American city. But there are different ways to inhabit a technological landscape. Elohel and Memory have resolved to live with it, or through it, in their own way. *Neptune Frost* is not opposed to high technology; indeed, it is deeply technophilic. But the film is also strongly concerned with the questions of who controls technology, how they use it, and for what ends. The film rejects both sides of an all-too-common binary. On the one hand, it rejects the idea that digital technology is a neutral tool that can be used indifferently for any end whatsoever. On the other hand, it also rejects the idea that a fixed set of social relations and forms of domination is irrevocably built into the technology. Technological inventions and developments radically alter ways of life. But the process is multi-sided: new forms of social life and social organization, such as the experiment of Digitaria, can lead to unanticipated technological mutations as well. This is why hacking is so important. In Digitaria, the technologies of communication and computation are not rejected; rather, they are hacked and hijacked and turned against their dominant modes of use.

Minute 31

Matalusa speaks of coltan as "the power in the Earth." He says that his brother Tekno "walked and dreamt with that power" before he was killed. Matalusa adds that he himself walks in order "to understand." As a chthonic power, the mineral exceeds (while still including) its technological use. The economic exploitation of Africa is also a terrestrial and cosmic usurpation of power. We are told of this insight only abstractly for now, but the rest of the film will explore, and show us, its ramifications. At this point, just as Matalusa speaks of walking, the movie switches back to the story of Neptune's travels. In a nighttime shot, we see her walking fast, with determination—as if to epitomize her earthly power. At first, we only see her legs, but as she continues striding away from the camera, we see her entire body from behind. She comes to a restaurant with electric lighting. She passes a table at which a man is seated. Inside the building, there is a long bar. A television behind the bar shows a soccer match, but then the image glitches. Neptune sits down at a table on the veranda just outside the entrance to the bar. She exchanges words with the waitress: "How's it?"—"Shining"—"Say what?"—"Unanimous Goldmine." This ritual of greeting will be repeated many times throughout the rest of the movie. The phrase "unanimous goldmine" implies wealth and plenty that are shared by everyone. Big corporations expropriate the bounty and power of the earth, thereby privatizing wealth for themselves and replacing universal affluence with privation and scarcity. Neptune and Matalusa, and also Elohel and Memory, all strive in their own ways to undo this situation and universalize abundance.

Minute 32

Neptune asks the waitress for "zingaro and beer." Since there is electricity in the restaurant, Neptune is able to get the beer cold—unlike Matalusa in the forest enclave. A man watches Neptune from his seat at the bar, his back turned to the television set that is still glitching. The waitress brings out a bottle of beer and pours it into a tall glass for Neptune. She drinks it avidly, as we see in medium close-up. The man at the bar comes out onto the veranda, stands at Neptune's table, and they exchange "Unanimous Goldmine" greetings.

Minute 33

The man is wearing a white sports jacket over a purple shirt. With a perfunctory "may I?", he sits down at the table across from Neptune. He introduces himself; his name is Innocent. He tells her that he is "just passing through." When he asks her, in turn, where she has come from, she evasively replies that "I am traveling from death to other passageways." It is evident that she doesn't entirely trust him. Nonetheless, he accepts this answer as if it made sense to him. Then he follows up by asking if she has come from the capitol, from the university, where (as we already know) student protests are going on. Neptune does not answer. Innocent leans in and whispers, warning her to be careful, because "the Authority's henchmen are everywhere." Throughout the scene, we see the two of them in a standard shot/reverse shot alternation. Innocent looks longingly at Neptune, clearly interested in picking her up. She looks back at him warily.

Minute 34

The shot/reverse shot alternation continues, and Innocent continues to speak softly about government repression. An election is coming up, but "we already know who will win." Neptune still does not answer any of Innocent's insinuations. In a broader shot, the waitress brings Neptune her meal. Zingaro is goat meat on skewers, particularly the intestines. Neptune avidly eats her food in medium close-up; she must be quite hungry. Innocent watches her and talks a bit more. It is difficult for me to make sense of Innocent. He seems a bit

FIGURE 7 Neptune Frost *directed by Saul Williams and Anisia Uzeyman* © *Kino Lorber 2021. All rights reserved.*

shifty and unreliable, belying his name; but it is hard to pin him down in any way.

Minute 35

Neptune apologizes for saying so little. She is hungry because "the journey has been long." Innocent responds with a joking aphorism: "one who swallows a whole coconut trusts his anus." They both laugh. The film returns to showing us a broader shot of the whole table, with the entrance to the bar and the television (still glitching) in the background. Two policemen—wearing the pink shirts and sinister face masks that we have seen before, in Minute 11, and also carrying machine guns—come to the bar. They glance at Neptune and Innocent for a moment and then walk inside. They ask the waitress why the television isn't working properly, and she apologizes and promises to "check the satellite." Such is the extent of globalization; local glitches may occur, but nothing is truly beyond the network's reach. Innocent quietly suggests to Neptune that he should pay her restaurant bill for her, presumably so that she does not arouse suspicion from the cops; she can pay him back once they get outside.

Minute 36

Having paid the bill, Innocent and Neptune leave the restaurant and walk together through the night. He is carrying her bag. At first, an orange tint permeates the night; this glow presumably derives from the restaurant's electricity. But as they walk along, they move into a considerably darker zone. The moon shines near the horizon. Innocent sings a song, without accompaniment, about the precariousness of identity, whether his own or that of others. The song moves from the singer's sense of his insignificance in the larger cosmos to the ways that the soldiers and police demand to pin down his identity, to the claim that, despite (or because of) this insignificance, "I own the night." *Neptune Frost* is a movie with continually varying rhythms; here the rhythm is at its slowest and most relaxed. The scene is a sort of tone poem to the night, with its moods and rhythms, both lulling and mysterious. The lyrical effect is strong, in spite of any reservations we might have about Innocent's character and intentions.

Minute 37

Neptune and Innocent come into a bar. The room is illuminated mostly in blue, except behind the bar where the wall is more or less reddish. Alternations between blue and red, in largely dark scenes, are a repeated motif throughout the movie; they help to express the poetic fragility of the night. The bar does not seem all that different in atmosphere from the restaurant they were at previously. Once again there is a television behind the bar that once again shows a soccer game and once again repeatedly glitches. A shot of the television screen, with the game overlaid by horizontal bands in various colors, is accompanied by an electronic sonic motif (suggesting a level reached or an achievement unlocked) that we will hear a number of times, periodically, throughout the rest of the film. A barman provides beers for Neptune and Innocent; they both drink. An eerie repeating synthesizer motif plays on the soundtrack. Neptune asks Innocent, "are you running from something?"; he replies, "not exactly," but ominously adds that "whatever we are running from is running to us all." At this point, the images start to appear in slow motion, though the sound is not affected. Neptune seems to be overcome by the drink; she staggers and falls forward, toward Innocent, before righting herself. Everything becomes blurry and out of focus: not only the figures of Neptune and Innocent but also the reddish lighting behind the bar and the glitch lines of the television. Neptune's and Innocent's bodies seem to sway in continuing slow motion. Has Neptune become extremely drunk all of a sudden? Or has Innocent slipped something into her drink? We do not really know. But our suspicions are aroused because—as also happened in Minute 22—Neptune's experience is now being rendered through a subjective camera, with visual distortions that match her psychological state.

Minute 38

The distortions of the previous minute continue, suggesting Neptune's fuzzy mental state. The screen is blurry, out of focus, and quite dark. Fragmentary slow-motion images of Neptune and Innocent are superimposed over one another. This sequence almost has the look of a semiabstract impressionist painting (only with slow, dreamlike movement). Muted reds and blues are played off against one another. Innocent and Neptune leave the bar and walk into the night. Neptune is unsteady, and Innocent holds on to her and guides her so she does not fall. The screen is nearly black until Innocent's hand and arm fill the frame as he lights a candle; they have evidently gone indoors again. On the soundtrack, the eerie repeating synthesizer motif is replaced by a fast, polyrhythmic drum'n'bass number, synthesized rhythms with fragmentary choral vocals. Innocent leans Neptune against a wall and moves in to kiss her.

Minute 39

As happens several times over the course of the movie, the combination of darkness and quick cuts makes it difficult to determine exactly what happens. The lighting varies wildly from second to second; at times, we can barely see the profiles of Innocent and Neptune, at other times they are almost violently illuminated. Innocent hugs and caresses Neptune;

she seems to reciprocate. Innocent lifts Neptune's dress and reaches underneath; a moment later, he stares at her in shock. This would seem to suggest that he finds out that her anatomy is not conventionally or entirely female. We don't really know any more than this; presumably Neptune is "intersex," but we are not given any information to specify what this means. A bit of political context is relevant here. Several East African countries have recently passed harsh anti-gay legislation at the instigation of evangelical Christian missionaries from the United States (Gates 2022; Global Health Justice 2023; Leonard 2023). In Rwanda, where the film was shot, sexual activities between same-sex people remain legal; however, marriage is officially defined as the union between a man and a woman (Wikipedia 2024d). Uzeyman says in an interview that she and Williams made "a conscious decision . . . a political decision" not to be too specific, given the political situation when they were shooting the film, since "not everywhere is the same" (Williams 2022). In any case, with his expectations apparently violated, Innocent angrily grabs Neptune; they struggle for a moment. Neptune harshly pushes Innocent away, breaks free of him, and runs out of the house and then through the night. We can barely see her red dress through the darkness; the camera tracks along with her, right to left, in a series of shots as she runs. Occasional blurry lights flash by. She does not say anything as she runs, but on the soundtrack we non-diegetically hear Neptune singing the same song that Innocent sang in Minute 36. The lyrics are about questioning one's own identity. But Neptune sings with much more urgency than Innocent did. This is in part because he was singing *a cappella*, softly and without projection, expressing a sort of detached skepticism. Neptune's voice, by contrast, is louder, and her expression is more dramatic; also, her singing is accompanied by droning instrumental lines and skittering drum'n'bass percussion. Neptune knows that her own identity, and therefore the extent to which others will accept her, is insecure and hanging in the balance.

Minute 40

Neptune continues to run, barely visible on the screen, and the camera continues to track alongside her, right to left. Neptune continues to sing on the soundtrack. Her running slows down, as does the moving camera; the song slows down as well, concluding with the repeated line, "I own the night!" Finally, Neptune and the camera tracking her both come to a stop. The musical accompaniment fades out as well. The screen is nearly all black. At this point there is a cut, although it is nearly invisible in the darkness. Now we can just barely discern a different figure, a person we have not seen before. The new figure seems to be male, and he is wearing a blue cape with a hood, in contrast to Neptune's red dress. Also, his direction of motion is the opposite of Neptune's: he moves into the frame from screen left, and he faces and tries to move toward screen right. But it takes us a moment to discern this. This gives us an instance of another surprising and unique editing effect in *Neptune Frost*. A cut from one location and sequence to another forces us to entirely reorient our attention, but the change is not immediately evident to our eyes. We are only able to realize retrospectively, after a few moments, that now things are different.

Minute 41

The man in the blue cloak seems to have reached an obstruction, although it is invisible in the dark. He pushes with his hands but only feels a barrier. He moves his hands over the obstruction, feeling his way, and finally he discovers a gap lower down. He stoops and passes through the barrier. It is hard to interpret what is happening here, in the dark, and for the first time. But we will encounter this invisible barrier several more times in the course of the film, during the daytime, when other people seek to enter the refuge of Digitaria. The obstruction is a bit like the semipermeable membrane of a biological cell: it creates a protected enclosure, separating the hackers' refuge from the rest of the world, but still allowing a certain degree of entry. On the soundtrack, the man's passage through the barrier is accompanied by a short electronic motif that sounds like the music marking an accomplishment—or a movement to the next level—in a video game; it is an expansion of the motif we previously heard when the television was glitching in Minute 37. On the other side of the barrier, it is too dark to see clearly. But several people are sitting around a fire, fanning the flames and feeding it with pieces of junk. Greetings are exchanged: "Unanimous Goldmine." There seems to be a woman with a baby strapped to her back. The verbal exchanges between the people around the fire and the newcomer are nervous and fragmentary. The man apologetically says that he is worried that he was followed. The camera moves unsteadily back and forth in front of the fire. The man asks whether it is safe here.

Minute 42

Memory responds to the man's question by reproaching him for playing "mind games." He apologizes, saying that such deceptions have saved his life. His name is Psychology (Trésor Niyongabo), and he has fled from the police and from the capitol. He speaks of the student protests. We see flashback footage similar to what we saw in Minute 11: students, with white shirts and yellow backpacks, running down a corridor and raising their fists in protest. Psychology starts singing and playing a lute as he tells of the violence with which the Authority met the demonstrations. Will Connor and Rich Cooper note, however, that we are not actually hearing the sound of a lute. Rather, we hear "the sound of a synthesizer. The sequenced notes employ large steps that would probably not be possible ergonomically for human hands to play on an acoustic lute." This sort of hybridity is central to *Neptune Frost* on every level. As Connor and Cooper put it, the movie works "to deconstruct boundaries, oppositions, juxtapositions, and the systems of control that create such binaries in the first place." Saul Williams comes from the United States, but he "returns to the Motherland with diasporic sound effects that disrupt modern visions of Africa" (Connor and Cooper 2025).

Minute 43

Psychology continues singing his account of what happened in the capitol. He is seated near the fire, in a circle with Memory and the others. There is continual cutting between his playing and singing in the present and the flashbacks to the confrontation between the police and the student protesters. Once again, we see the pink-shirted police from behind, as they form a line in order to push back against the chaotic crowd of students chanting slogans and waving signs. Psychology also says that the Authority cut off mass media (radio, television, internet) in their attempt to stop the protests. Top-down media work to create uniformity, suppress dissent, and program people's possible responses.

Minute 44

Psychology's song continues. We see additional flashback shots of the police confronting protesters, breaking into classrooms and private rooms, and shining their flashlights at people, both male and female, who hold their hands up in surrender. The police enter private rooms and make arrests. We also see Psychology deciding to flee, gathering his things, and slipping on a pink dress. We have already seen how the police seek to enforce order of all sorts, including the order of binary gender. Psychology appears to be male, rather than intersex (whatever that is taken to mean) like Neptune. But perhaps, by fleeing in drag, he hopes to deflect police scrutiny. In any case, the flashback shows us Psychology leaving the university under cover of darkness. When we return from these flashbacks to the scene of Psychology singing and playing his instrument, while he is surrounded by a circle of women, it has started to get light: the night in which he fled is almost over.

Minute 45

Psychology completes his song. The music (ostensibly from the lute) continues for several seconds as the camera pans upward through trees and into the lightening sky. There is another transition here: a cut to a different scene: a pastoral one. Now, in full daytime, we see rows of crops, as tall as human bodies. The crops are tended by nuns dressed in white from head to toe, including cowls over their heads. Two of the nuns turn toward a shack, or a barn, standing amid the crops; they go inside and find Neptune asleep on the straw that covers the floor.

Minute 46

The elderly leader of the nuns is played by Cécile Kayirebwa: she is a celebrated Rwandan singer and poet (Gates 2022), and her "special participation" in the film is singled out for thanks in the credits. The nun awakens Neptune and addresses her as *Chana*. But Neptune replies that "Chana" is her mother's name. The nun explains that Chana was her best friend before the war and that Neptune closely resembles her. Chana "had a baby just before the war: a little boy." But in the course of the war, Chana and the nun were separated. Neptune accepts this story and says nothing of her altered gender. The two of

FIGURE 8 Neptune Frost *directed by Saul Williams and Anisia Uzeyman* © *Kino Lorber 2021. All rights reserved.*

them are now seated, out of doors, on a log. The nun speaks, and Neptune, right beside her, looks at her avidly. We see the other nuns tending to the plants in the field behind them. The elder nun begins to sing, *a cappella*, about her memories of Chana and of their friendship. The other nuns stop working in order to listen to their leader's song and then they walk slowly up a slope toward her. They are all mesmerized by her singing, or perhaps by the content of her recollections. This is an exemplary point in the film, one of many in which the focus is not upon furthering the action, but rather upon unfolding, and dwelling within, a certain emotional configuration. Here is a moment of strong affective resonance in the course of a conflation of past and present, or of memory and desire: Chana giving birth before the war, Neptune being reborn after the war is finally over, and the nun, with her song, bringing both of these experiences together. In *Neptune Frost*, we cannot simply revert to the past; but neither can we overlook all the ways that the past still resonates in the present.

Minute 47

The nun's song continues. The camera executes a long horizontal pan, moving right from the other nuns to the older nun singing to Neptune, who faces her and listens with concentration. The camera continues to pan to the right, past both of them, until it encounters two more nuns who are walking up a slope—at which point the camera reverses direction and pans back to the left as the nuns pass behind Neptune and the chief nun. There are several separate shots of the elderly nun caressing Neptune, moving her hands over the skin of Neptune's arms as she continues her song. This is followed by another long horizontal pan, from right to left, showing the nuns all in a line listening. I dwell on the camera movements here because we do not encounter anything quite like them elsewhere in the film. This is a privileged moment in Neptune's journey, one that she and we may well wish to preserve in memory—even as it passes, as all such moments must. In her song, the chief nun stresses compassion and forgiveness, and speaks of leaving her songs as a gift to later generations.

Minute 48

As the nun's song concludes, the camera moves upward, past the trees and into the sky: a movement of punctuation and transition that we have seen a number of times before. The nun's final words offer us healing and transformation: "In the end, I will heal from what happened before the war." As the camera soars upward a new musical motif replaces her voice, picking up her melody: it sounds like it comes from the mbira family of African musical instruments. The film cuts from a static shot of the sky to a pan right to left through the branches of trees in the forest. This camera movement is coordinated with the mbira music on the soundtrack; the pan is formally similar to, but much faster than, those that accompanied the nun's song. Another cut brings us back to the hacker encampment. Elohel is trying, without much success, to fix the various technical devices lying around at the e-waste site. Like the Wheel Man earlier in the film, Elohel is something of a *bricoleur*. Claude Lévi-Strauss describes the *bricoleur* as a deliberately unsystematic pragmatist who takes whatever materials can be found, in their very fragility and impermanence, as opportunities "for renewing or enriching his [*sic*] stock, or for maintaining it with leftovers from earlier constructions and destructions" (Lévi-Strauss 2021). Elohel perseveres in this, even though there is still no electricity. Psychology hands her one of the plastic hexagonal wireless devices that we have seen earlier in the film, but she cannot get it to function. Psychology says that, nonetheless, "all these things seem to connect to something . . . it's a strange feeling, like being cut off from the world." Memory passes by just at this moment; she is someone who always looks for different perspectives, and so she offhandedly asks Psychology: "which world?" With this exchange, the film moves to define the hacker encampment as what Michel Foucault calls a *heterotopia*: one of "these different spaces, these other places, a kind of contestation, both mythical and real, of the space in which we live." Foucault's word *contestation* implies both opposition and connection; where traditional utopias are entirely separate from the actual everyday world, heterotopias remain obscurely connected to it. Places like libraries, old age homes, pirate ships, and even prisons can work as heterotopias. They hold themselves apart from the rest of the world, but they remain very much *composed by* the very societies from which they separate themselves. The key point, for Foucault, is that "heterotopias always presuppose a system of opening and closing that isolates them and makes them penetrable at the same time" (Foucault 1998). The invisible barrier that surrounds Digitaria functions very much in this way. Digitaria offers a hope of escape from digital surveillance and control, but it also mobilizes digital technologies against the powers that usually wield them. Heterotopias put themselves at a distance from the everyday world, and from that distance they criticize the world and offer corrections to it. They both negate the everyday world, and yet remain in some sort of communication with it.

Minute 49

The screen becomes dark again. Alternations of light and dark, or of day and night, are one of the major organizing formal features of *Neptune Frost*. Matalusa is asleep; his hair is now festooned with metal spikes or wires, presumably scavenged from the surrounding e-waste. A voice calls out: "Mata! Mata!" It is the voice of Matalusa's brother Tekno, who was murdered in Minute 4. Matalusa stirs in his sleep; Tekno exhorts him to "Look!" A rock is slowly rotating in midair: this is the very rock of coltan for which Tekno was killed. Tekno tells Matalusa: "You see! We power the system. It is the same energy that flows through us." The energy that powers our cell phones comes from the earth and remains tied to the earth. This energy is intrinsic to the planet itself and to the people—like the coltan miners—who work upon, and work in, the earth. Matalusa's dream vision, in which his brother returns to life, combines wondrous mysticism with a Marxist conception of alienation and of the extraction of surplus value. I am reminded of a comment by Jordan Hoffman in his review of *Neptune Frost*: "Not since *Zabriskie Point* has [*sic*] psychedelia and Marxism worked together so effectively on screen" (Hoffman 2022). This is a surprising juxtaposition, but in many ways an apt one. The desert of Antonioni's film is, of course, quite different from the lush highland forest of *Neptune Frost*; but both films employ these locations, far from the cities of Los Angeles or of Kigali, in order to deploy phantasmatic visions of liberation. Both films similarly insist that there is no contradiction between the delirious aestheticism with which they display their images (and, in the case of *Neptune Frost*, sounds as well) and the thematic resonance of their calls for social and political revolution. At this point, nearly halfway through *Neptune Frost*, the visionary sequence ends with Matalusa waking up for real, still calling out Tekno's name as he did in the dream. This is followed by a cut to the white and red bird we have seen before, only this time flying from the left edge of the frame instead of from the right.

Minute 50

The bird gives way to long shots of Neptune, in her red dress, once again walking through the fields, in the same left-to-right direction, as if her motion were somehow coordinated with, or impelled by, that of the bird. The next shot, from extremely high above, shows her walking away from the camera on a yellow pathway that cuts across the green fields. This shot, in turn, dissolves into a much closer shot so that her entire body extends from the bottom to almost the top of the screen as she walks through the forest instead of the fields. Her direction

FIGURE 9 Neptune Frost *directed by Saul Williams and Anisia Uzeyman* © *Kino Lorber 2021. All rights reserved.*

of motion has now also switched its orientation: she walks from screen right to screen left. All this while, Neptune's voice-over narration speaks of "fear and longing, with no sense of belonging." But she goes on to say that such "dissonance . . . became a song in me." She explains that "what attempted to gender or 'boy' me" failed to have its intended effect and instead "set me free." This resonates with the previous scenes of Elohel's heterotopia and of Matalusa's dream; in all three cases, potentials drawn from situations of oppression are retooled into forms of liberation. Now that she is in the forest and relatively close to the camera, Neptune suddenly breaks into full-fledged song and dance, with direct singing replacing the offscreen voice-over, and with musical accompaniment on the soundtrack. This is the most vehement song we have heard thus far in the course of the movie. Neptune sings about the need to break away from hegemonic misunderstandings and distortions; she continues to move right to left, but she often faces toward, and stares directly at, the camera. Behind her, among the trees, we see two groups of backup dancers, whose costumes we recognize from earlier scenes in the movie: one group consists of white-shirted university students waving books, and the other group consists of pink-shirted policemen holding nightsticks. Needless to say, their presence in the forest is not actual or naturalistic but an expression and an example of the way that *Neptune Frost* revises and rearranges social and political reality in the closest the film comes to what in other musicals would be a full-fledged production number, or more accurately a music video sequence.

Minute 51

The musical accompaniment behind Neptune's song is thickened with percussion. She has finished singing, but her body continues to move rhythmically as she takes off her high-heeled shoes: the very ones that she had first put on her feet in

Minute 20, when she still presented as male. Neptune stares occasionally at the camera and then turns away from it, and, barefoot, walks further into the dark depths of the forest. After a moment, and as the percussion and minimal melody become less regular, the dark screen is filled with figures moving away from the camera just as Neptune did. We can barely make them out; only the white bundles they carry on their backs are discernible. We cut to a blurry, out-of-focus shot that resolves into a daytime scene of the forest, with the people we saw now visible as a group of men walking screen left to screen right through the trees and then turning toward the camera. They bump into Digitaria's invisible barrier, just as Psychology did in Minute 41. For me, there is something breathtaking about this moment of transition, or more generally about the several transitions of the previous three minutes of the film. We go from Psychology and Elohel's conversation about reusing digital detritus, to Matalusa's dream of his dead brother, to Neptune's trek through the forest, to the men finding the barrier that shields Digitaria. All these different groups of characters are exploring, each in their own ways, what Deleuze and Guattari call *lines of flight*: not just physical movements of departure and escape but also new articulations of possibility and hope (Deleuze and Guattari 1987). I think of this progression of scenes as a sort of intellectual montage: a complex association not just of shots but of sequences; as I have discussed previously regarding more immediate juxtapositions of image to image, the effect is to open up the world of the film (and its relation to the actual world) in a way that goes well beyond conventional continuity editing. At the same time, this arrangement works its resonances in a different way than Eisenstein ever did, though like Eisenstein's, Williams' and Uzeyman's practice of montage is both didactic and poetic.

Minute 52

Again, like Psychology before them, the men feel out the invisible barrier and eventually discover a gap lower down that allows them to crawl through. Spotting Matalusa, the men greet him and run toward him. They all squeeze together in a group hug. These are Matalusa's fellow coltan miners; they have been guided by dreams—apparently sent to them by the late Tekno—to join Matalusa in his forest refuge. There is all-round rejoicing. Matalusa still has the metal spikes woven into his hair that we previously saw when he dreamed of Tekno in Minute 49. He is also now wearing a remarkable e-waste costume, a jacket festooned with keys from discarded computer keyboards. He will continue to wear this jacket for the remainder of the film.

Minute 53

The miners credit Tekno with having taught them to understand the value of what they were digging up. Matalusa introduces his fellow (ex-)miners to Elohel and Memory. He says that he does not miss the labor of mining, but he misses the music. They all spontaneously start dancing to an *a cappella* call-and-response song about their labor: "The miner is the power source"—"Dig!". In the chorus, the miners sing that they are "Alone but not alone." Community comes from the combination of each individual's experiences of alienation and isolation. It's dark again. For a few seconds, the movie cuts to a location in the forest much further away from the group, so that we can only hear them singing in the distance. We are barely able to discern Neptune walking through the trees, from screen left to screen right.

Minute 54

A cut returns us to the group of miners, along with Elohel and Memory. The call-and-response high-volume singing continues, as does the dancing. Bodies bounce up and down in the dark. "Mining is music." This continues, or makes more explicit, a theme that is woven through the entire film. It goes back to Tekno's wonderment at the rock he has extracted in Minute 4 and the return of this rock, rotating in midair, in Matalusa's dream in Minute 49. Coltan is not just a thing of instrumental use for computer technology. It also has an intrinsic beauty all of its own, exemplifying the wealth of the land and of its people—once these can be freed from exploitation and expropriation by the West. The singing and dancing cease, and we cut back to a further-away, very dark shot of Neptune walking through the forest. We hear an electronic crackling and an eerie musical motif. Neptune looks up. The next shot shows a light source in the sky—perhaps the moon—which seems to turn pinkish in color and to expand. We cut back to the people who were previously singing and dancing; they also look up at the sky

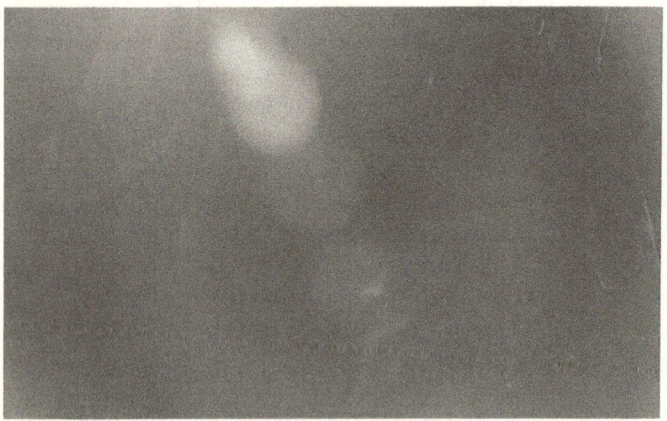

FIGURE 10 Neptune Frost *directed by Saul Williams and Anisia Uzeyman © Kino Lorber 2021. All rights reserved.*

and see the same expanding celestial light. Memory tells the miners to "Make a wish." We return to Neptune walking in the forest, heading toward the camera. Things are coming to a point of culmination: what the dialectical tradition might call a moment of condensation or even of fusion.

Minute 55

Neptune encounters the invisible barrier that guards Digitaria. With her hands, she feels it in front of her, just as the others did. But she is able to pass through it without having to stoop down. As she passes, we hear an expanded version of the electronic motif that accompanied the passage of the others. In addition, the whole screen brightens to pink for a moment and then subsides. As Neptune enters the refuge, her red dress is transformed: now it is metallic and glistening. It is impressive to see this as the camera passes down her body and up again. But it is still quite dark, so that Neptune's figure is barely visible; for this reason, the shot does not feel voyeuristic to me. Just after this, all of a sudden, electric lights blink and turn on. Fluorescent lights play over plants in what might be a greenhouse. The bodies of the dancers are no longer hidden in darkness; both Memory and Elohel look around themselves with delight. Even the plastic hexagonal wireless devices that we have seen several previous times in the movie start to work again. Neptune has somehow brought electrical power to the refuge; she actively provides the light, rather than being exhibitionistically illuminated by it.

Minute 56

People in the refuge react with excitement to the presence of electricity. Some of the men pick up and start playing musical instruments. Other people once again start dancing. Neptune's voice-over narration resumes: "I was plugged in. I felt the power coursing through me . . . I was where I was meant to be." She stands still in the middle of the action, and in the middle of the screen, and she looks around in wonder. As light strobes over her body, she remains present but not active, remarking that "this is an observation deck." At the risk of sounding simple-mindedly essentialistic, not to mention inverting temporal sequence, I want to say that this is the real thing of which the multicultural dance party in Zion in *The Matrix Reloaded* (The Wachowskis, 2003) is an empty simulacrum.

Minute 57

The music and dancing continue. Neptune still looks around at everything with wonder. Matalusa, dancing, tells Elohel: "It's all so much. I lost my brother a few days ago, and now I feel like I'm in another world." The singer sings the words, "martyr . . . loser," and Elohel tells Matalusa that "this is Matalusa Kingdom." The play on words—"Martin Luther King" becomes "Martyr, Loser, King" and also "Matalusa King"—resonates throughout the rest of the movie. I have already mentioned how this phrase, with its multiple resonances, has its origin in Saul Williams' album *MartyrLoserKing*, which is a precursor to the movie and contains earlier versions of many of its songs. Or else, we might better say that the album stands alongside the movie as part of a vaster (and most likely, never-to-be-completed) multimedia project. In any case, the musicians continue to play, the people continue to dance, and Neptune continues to watch. The song turns into a raucous call-and-response: "Anger . . . Self-control . . . Tolerance . . . Wisdom . . . Ecstasy." These are the stages of self-transformation, perhaps.

Minute 58

The music and dancing continue. But the volume decreases, so that the dance music is only background, as Neptune and Matalusa, in reverse shots, notice one another and stare at one another. They seem mutually mesmerized. The camera glides along with them, in separate shots, as they both walk through the crowd of dancers. Finally, they reach one another, face-to-face, with Neptune on screen left looking right and Matalusa on screen right looking left back at her. Their dialogue is presented in traditional shot-reverse shot format. Matalusa proclaims to her: "That is one way of telling a story." Neptune asks: "Is this the interface?" Matalusa responds: "This is a dream." He says that he is "dreaming," and she responds: "Not I." Perhaps this is because he has been disoriented for the entire movie, ever since his brother was murdered in the opening minutes. Neptune, on the other hand, has gone through a series of events in which she threw off illusions and

FIGURE 11 Neptune Frost *directed by Saul Williams and Anisia Uzeyman* © *Kino Lorber 2021. All rights reserved.*

false constructions. In any case, after this shot-reverse shot exchange, we finally see Matalusa and Neptune facing one another in a single shot. They are backlit by fluorescent lights and slightly out-of-focus walls and greenery. We briefly saw what might have been a greenhouse in Minute 55; now they seem to be within such a building, even though previous shots suggested that the dance party was taking place outside, in the middle of the forest. Once again, this does not strike the viewer as a violation of continuity but rather as its intensification. The lighting remains consistent from shot to shot throughout this sequence, and the change in location works subliminally to amplify the emotional weight of Neptune's and Matalusa's meeting.

Minute 59

The camera returns to shot-reverse shot alternation, as Neptune and Matalusa continue to talk. Neptune gently caresses Matalusa's face. They stare enraptured at one

FIGURE 12 Neptune Frost *directed by Saul Williams and Anisia Uzeyman* © *Kino Lorber 2021. All rights reserved.*

another, and Neptune's voice-over explains the meaning of the greeting that we have already heard a number of times: "Unanimous Goldmine is the greeting of the resource rich, who face a world beholden to the currency of our depletion. This golden salute elevates the vibration of metallic injustice to the threshold of planetary sustenance." At this point, Neptune's voice-over is not just a form of narration but also, and beyond this, a kind of poetic catalyst, giving universal resonance to what are otherwise just single events. "When I beheld Matalusa," she continues, "the greeting took on new dimensions." As Neptune continues to explain, the camera roams around the space, panning left and then right again. Although we hear the music of the party continuing in the background, through a cinematic manipulation of time, the physical action seems to have stopped. The camera pans over a motionless tableau of bodies wearing garments of different colors. Finally, the camera returns to Neptune and Matalusa, but it has moved to the other side of the line in which they are facing one another, so that now Matalusa is on screen left, and Neptune is on screen right. After a moment of this, the camera starts roving again through the crowd of stilled bodies. Neptune tells us, in her voice-over, that she is overwhelmed: "I attempted to speak but was struck by the millions of conversations streaming through me. An influx of information. Code, streams of light, virtual lanes of traffic becoming more legible. Data, wa wa wa." (The final syllables "wa wa wa" are not rendered in the subtitles, but I record this inflection of Neptune's voice because it was so clearly audible.) This is a moment of overwhelming insight and influx of energy. I do not know if this is a good parallel or analogy, but I am reminded of one of my favorite moments in all of cinema: the scene (there are actually two of them) in Jean-Luc Godard's *Two or Three Things I Know About Her* when Marina Vlady proclaims, "It was as if I were the world and the world were me." Neptune has become a universal conductor, transducer, and capacitator; her body and consciousness are the monadic switching point through which everything digital and electronic must pass. She plays the same role for the entire worldwide network that anodes of coltan-derived tantalum play for individual electronic devices. This is not the digital *as opposed to* the analog or to the physical; rather, Neptune seems to concentrate, in her very being, the density of a world that is equally embodied and informatic. As the coltan miners have already shown us, materiality and information are two parallel attributes of the same Spinozian substance. The order and connection of information is the same as the order and connection of physical bodies.

Minute 60

As Neptune's voice-over continues, the screen itself starts glitching. Lurid false colors flare out momentarily; bodies are reduced to ray-traced outlines; the screen is overwritten with moving patterns of bent lines, diamonds, and trapezoids. Electronic hums and pulses of noise play behind Neptune's words as she feels herself becoming "Moses on the mountaintop . . . The burning bush was a firewall . . . Encrypted messages on a tablet." All of a sudden, the electronic noise and visual interference are cut off. Instead, we see the whole crowd of people in the refuge, standing in the dark. They clap their hands, and sway, jump, and dance in place. Elohel chants, and all of them join her in a chorus. They express their refusal to be silenced or to be exploited by the West. Instead, they insist that "the future is my home, it all came from here." Some music is added on the soundtrack, but a sense of presence and solidarity in the here and now predominates, in sharp contrast to the electronic glitches just before. I am dazzled by the way that the film switches between glitch digital electronics and unvarnished analog presentation. Both of these are inescapable dimensions, woven into the fabric of the world.

Minute 61

The chanting and dancing continue. Call-and-response singing points up all the political and economic connections between Africa and the West. Whether computers or guns are at issue, the refrain insists that "you know we paid for it all." This eventually shifts into a warning: "You'll never touch my love." In the latter portion of this minute, the two different regimes of images from the previous minute are now combined or overlaid upon one another. The digital-electronic glitches resume, but now they are composited with, and pasted over, the continuing images and sounds of the people dancing. These digital images are ghostly: they fade into impalpability almost as soon as they appear. We glimpse a Western newscaster for a moment: she is the only white person to appear in the entire movie. The subtitles here show the words of the newscasts: "The Prime Minister spoke today." The scene's digital overlays also include words (in all capitals) glimpsed for a moment, such as "GLOBAL NETWORK." All this reminds us how even the most abstract digital transmissions are still premised upon the materiality of human bodies, that is to say, upon their labor and their recreation. We might even say that the networks are parasitic upon corporeal human energy. But there is nothing here of what Louis Althusser disparagingly called an *expressive totality*, "in which all the elements are total parts, each expressing the internal unity of the totality" (Althusser 1976). Rather, the network has its own internal and inconsistent logic; it is simply *spread over* the bodies and energies whose specificities it ignores and from which it violently extracts its own capacities for domination and destruction.

Minute 62

The violent digital overlays upon the dancing in the refuge continue, indeed intensify. On the soundtrack, these digital incursions take the form of bursts of white noise. Then the digital intrusions are all, once again (as already happened in Minute 60), instantaneously cut off. This is possible because digital forms have sharp and distinct edges, whereas analog forms do not. The dance music continues, but fades into the background. Matalusa introduces Neptune (whose name he only now learns) to Memory. Elohel finds that her plastic hexagonal wireless device is now fully operative; she is ecstatic about this, but she does not understand how or why it happened.

Minute 63

The dancing continues; the music returns to the foreground. Matalusa starts rapping. He emphasizes gender fluidity: "Met this girl on Friday night.... Purple satin bra and tights / That's what I was wearing." This all leads up to: "We broke the code. Let's make noise." The chorus simply repeats the words "Girl Boy Girl Boy" multiple times (this particular line is rapped in French slang: "mec meuf meuf mec meuf"). All the people in the refuge are dancing, in various combinations; the camera shows their bodies glistening out of the darkness. I have already mentioned how, throughout the movie, Williams and Uzeyman are especially attentive to the problem of properly lighting dark skin. As Robert Daniels writes, in classical Hollywood, "lighting and cinematography techniques have traditionally privileged white actors, to the detriment of how their Black co-stars appeared onscreen." In order to avoid such a default white look, Williams and Uzeyman "took plenty of risks in their lighting by mixing distinct complementary colors and by playing with shadows in inspiring ways: The skin often adopts a pink, orange, even green glow that speaks to the political and personal transformations experienced by the characters" (Daniels 2022). Uzeyman herself notes how "the characters emit a certain quality of light"; the aim was "to film dark skin tones with a kind of luminescence. It became less a matter of projecting something onto the characters than bringing it out of them, so that they appeared to glow" (Marcks 2022). I think that Uzeyman's emphasis upon bringing something out from the characters rather than projecting something upon them is essential to the aesthetics of *Neptune Frost*. It allows for an expansion of references and associations; it is a way of breaking the code and opening up the uncoded processes of noise.

Minute 64

Matalusa continues to rap. Now the theme is changing the code, changing the books: hacking, in short, though he does not use that word here. Matalusa's rap combines phrases in African languages with ones in English, French, and even Portuguese. He urges us to "Think Black, Think Gay," and to look at things and experience them directly—as opposed to the hegemonic "they," who "Think White, Think Straight," and who only believe what they read in books. During a respite between verses, the music is backgrounded for a few seconds. Neptune and Matalusa continue to dance. She looks at him carefully; then he looks back at her in a reverse shot, still dancing. A third shot shows her looking in his direction, avidly and with wonder. Caught up in her thoughts, she has gone still. Many of the film's most important moments hang upon looks and gestures, which are contained within the narrative, but which seem to have their own autonomy. While the words of Matalusa's rap express many of the movie's themes, the actors' bodily gestures, and the looks that Neptune and Matalusa exchange—together with the intricacies of lighting and the articulation of spatial volumes—are what give *Neptune Frost* its mysterious emotional charge. We continue to ponder the question of just who Neptune is and what she accomplishes (perhaps without entirely realizing it) through the miracle of her presence.

Minute 65

The dance and the rap continue for part of this minute. Everything is ambiguous and reversible: "Words are sometimes prisons, sometimes prisms from the way you look." But Neptune is still standing motionless. When the camera passes over her, the music again is backgrounded. Neptune's voice-over returns to dominate the soundtrack. She speaks wonderingly of the earth "from an outsider's perspective": everything seems "split" and incomplete to her. However, she insists that "I was in control of my instrument, on a dance floor, free of fear." After this, the digital glitches we have seen earlier start pulsing again: they play over Neptune's image as she stands motionless. Once again, we see how Neptune has become a focal point through whom the global computation and communication networks pass. Neptune stares at the camera, raises her head to look upward, then lowers it to look straight at the camera again. She is right at the center of the screen, as the glitches continue to flash both over her and behind her. This is the moment of Neptune's apotheosis. But then, for a few seconds, Neptune's triumphant image and the background party music are suddenly replaced by sustained electronic tones and the vision of a ball spinning, with blurry images, at the center of an otherwise entirely dark frame. This, in its turn, is replaced by an uneven but pulsing pinkish field, such as we previously saw, associated with Neptune's power, in Minutes 54 and 55. A moment later, the electronic glitches return, as does Neptune's voice-over.

Minute 66

As glitch lines and pinkish pulses of light fill the screen, Neptune tells us in her voice-over that she is "a bird flying high over a mountain of data...a sea of information coded in spiral." Slowly changing electronic drones play on the soundtrack, replacing the dance music. Neptune holds the position of what Deleuze and Guattari call "absolute survey": a sort of perception that is entirely immanent to what is being perceived (Deleuze and Guattari 1994). Neptune overlooks a "mountain" or "sea" of information, but this is because she herself is a crucial node of all the information flows. After this, we see a montage of images—some familiar from before and some not—while an electronic monotone plays softly on the soundtrack. There are stacks of computer monitors amid vegetation, on the back wall of Neptune's hut. The camera discovers a forested island in the middle of the sea. Neptune is lying on the floor, falling asleep, with Matalusa right behind her, in shots that have a heavy reddish tinge. One shot gives us a close-up of an intricate earring that she wears. There are flashbacks to the Wheel Man; he is working on some contraption, but in daylight rather than darkness. Indeed, the party has ended, and we have somehow transitioned from night to day. The camera glides through the upper reaches of the forest, passing over foliage and flowers, especially a tree with bright red blooms.

Minute 67

We see the revelers from the past night, spread out asleep on the ground, amid piles of high-tech detritus. Psychology wakes up, stares at his hexagonal wireless device, and runs—in slow motion—to awaken Elohel and tell her about his connection. The "I-FI" (a neologism, presumably instead of "Wi-Fi") is suddenly working for everybody. The same electronic motif as when people cross the barrier protecting Digitaria plays on

FIGURE 13 Neptune Frost *directed by Saul Williams and Anisia Uzeyman © Kino Lorber 2021. All rights reserved.*

the soundtrack. The camera swish pans back to the original group of sleepers, all of whom are in the process of waking up, standing up, and looking with surprise at their devices. But what is most amazing, as one of the miners tells Elohel, is "not the signal" but rather "the content." All the ex-miners start to sing about how they now "own the Internet."

Minute 68

The song continues, everyone raising their arms and dancing in place. The people in the refuge have "five million followers"— no, make that "five billion followers." Elohel leads them all in a chant of how their "roach egg economy" is spreading everywhere (this phrase seems to imply a swarming and multiplication from below). Meanwhile, Neptune and Matalusa, inside their hut, awaken. Computer monitors are still pulsing in the background. Now we find out the "content" that is the source of all the excitement. Memory comes into the hut and—against the background of multiple pulsing computer monitors—informs Neptune and Matalusa that they have "inspired a world-wide trend. . . . Neptune has found a way to capture the world's attention, and we're the most talked about thing on the virtual face of the planet." Everything has changed overnight due to Neptune's arrival in the forest refuge and her connection with Matalusa.

Minute 69

The conversation in the hut continues. The world is talking about the hacking exploits of "MARTYR LOSER KING." Not only has Neptune plugged into the worldwide network but the network has also anxiously reacted. Memory, Neptune, and Matalusa worry about whether the hack can be traced back to them. Neptune says that, for the moment, Russia and China are being blamed. But the point, she adds, is "not what I see, but what I see through." It is not the literal information itself that matters, but rather the movements and the connections that are

FIGURE 14 Neptune Frost *directed by Saul Williams and Anisia Uzeyman © Kino Lorber 2021. All rights reserved.*

thereby enabled. We see Neptune's face in extreme close-up at this point, emphasizing the power that flows through her. "But what I see here," Neptune says and pauses; Memory completes her sentence: "is a gateway?" So much of *Neptune Frost* seems to be about crossing thresholds, though without any definite revelation of what might happen once we have gotten entirely through the gateway. At this point, we hear the cry of the bird from before, and we see another brief shot of the bird flying on the right edge of the screen. Memory brings it into the hut and introduces it to Neptune and Matalusa. Its name is Frost (thus explaining the second half of the film's title). Neptune has not met the bird before, "but I believe we are acquainted." She finds it familiar, just as she found Matalusa familiar, even though they had only previously met in the dream vision of the Wheel Man. The connections continue to proliferate. Africans have been exploited by the West, but ultimately Africans are at the heart of the global network; everything about it is grounded in what they do. But how far does this network extend? Matalusa looks both startled and abstracted; Memory tells him, "you look like you've seen a witch." Matalusa responds that his mother was called a witch, but that this is not what bothers him now.

Minute 70

Matalusa explains his preoccupied air by telling Neptune and Memory about his past. We see Matalusa telling his story in close-up, with occasional brief reaction shots of the others. Matalusa recounts that his brother Tekno was given that name because their father was dazzled by the promises of technology. But Matalusa and Tekno had to remain in hiding during the war, and when it finally ended, they found that they had lost their family's land. They could only stay if they worked in the mines, digging up "technology"—or so the bosses told them. So they stayed and took on the backbreaking work of mining coltan. The old story of alienation, expropriation, and exploitation unfolds once again. Memory responds that at least Matalusa is safe now, in the refuge.

Minute 71

But Neptune immediately responds, warning them that they are not really safe. Outside of the refuge, the exploiters still control everything. Neptune starts to sing about how everything is interconnected and controlled by those in power so that we are all, willy-nilly, "down for some ignorance." Memory takes up the song, and then Matalusa does as well. The song is interrupted when Psychology enters the hut to tell Matalusa the news, but the reports are already there, on the multiple computer monitors on the back wall of the hut. Russia and China have denied responsibility for the worldwide hack, "the greatest breach of the virtual age."

Minute 72

As a new musical motif starts playing, Memory explains to Psychology that the "connection" between Neptune and Matalusa is the driver of everything that is happening. They all leave the hut; Matalusa is carried in celebration by the other miners. We see this both from far above and from ground level. When the others put Matalusa back on his feet, he tells them that "Technology was the name of my brother, and it's Technology that guides us today. . . . They use our blood and sweat to communicate with each other, but have never heard our voice." At least this has been the case "until now," as another miner replies. Since Africans originate the technology, at least in the sense of pulling it from the ground, they should be able to reclaim it.

Minute 73

Matalusa continues declaiming: "we do the work that is hidden behind their screens." The power of coltan runs through the people who extract it. "We have no authority," Matalusa says, "but maybe now we have a voice . . . And vision!" Now, perhaps, they can force the Authority to listen to them. We see the action from above: Matalusa stands at the center of a circle of miners as he makes his speech. They all respond to his statements with shouts of approval; even without music, this is a sort of call-and-response. However, despite their new awareness, all is not well. When music finally does play on the soundtrack, the bodies of the miners start shaking, all at once. It is as if some electric current that they are unable to control were coursing through them. The miners jerk their arms and legs, while their heads are bowed down. Matalusa is the only one not affected; he looks around in puzzlement and worry. Meanwhile, behind Matalusa, an enormous gray rock, with tiny blue lights embedded in it, floats in midair. This is reminiscent, on a far greater scale, of the rock rotating in midair in Matalusa's dream in Minute 49.

Minute 74

The shaking of the miners' bodies continues as the camera pans through the group, from one body to the next. Whereas early in the movie, in Minutes 6 and 7, while the miners were actually at work they managed to transform their labor into a kind of dance, here the inverse occurs: even though they have been liberated from the mine, their bodily spasms show them still to be entrapped, zombie-like, by the harsh rhythms of backbreaking labor. This strange scene perhaps helps to make us acutely aware that—contrary to the common ideology of the digital—we cannot escape from the intensities of corporeal embodiment. Our mobile phones and other digital devices "are all light and clean," as Donna Haraway once famously put it, "because they are nothing but signals, electromagnetic waves, a section of a spectrum" (Haraway 1991). And yet, the miners here remind us—as the movie as a whole continually does—that coltan mining, in its violence and its grubby materiality, provides the raw material that is needed in order to drive these impalpable signals. Haraway herself is one of the first to point out that under the sway of these new inventions, people of all genders are increasingly *feminized*, which means "to be made extremely vulnerable; able to be disassembled, reassembled, exploited as a reserve labor force; seen less as workers than as servers; subjected to time arrangements on and of the paid job that make a mockery of a limited workday; leading an existence that always borders on being obscene, out of place, and reducible to sex" (Haraway 1991). This situation is still the background experience of the coltan miners, despite their having escaped to Digitaria. We are still trapped at the threshold. Matalusa himself is not free of this condition. As the general shaking continues, his own body starts to spasm as well, but in a slightly different way: it looks as if he is desperately trying to expel something from his system. Finally, he pukes out the beginning of a new song: "Brothers gone, M-WIndows On! Sisters gone, Google On!"

Minute 75

Matalusa continues to sing, quite vehemently, and the other miners continue to sway. Matalusa's song swells into a full-fledged dystopian vision of how local destruction in the periphery is required to power the high-technology capitalist world. There is one shot, from above, where an electronically generated blue rectangle outlines Matalusa's head, suggesting that he is being scanned by software and marked as a target. The chorus of Matalusa's song is plaintive: "Nobody knows I'm alone, tell them I need somebody." But there seems to be no way out, as Matalusa continues to sing his harsh vision of ruin at increasing volume. He even confronts us, the listeners and viewers, for our complicity in this cycle of exploitation and destruction: "You think I don't know that you're bad and wrong? Welcome Mister Nobody."

Minute 76

Matalusa still continues his song. Parts of his face and body have an electronic red glow. As Matalusa comes to the climax of his song—chanting "Fuck Mr. Google" and thrusting his extended middle finger right into the camera—the image breaks apart. There seems to be a glitch, so that a few seconds of the song, right in the middle of Matalusa's curse, get played a second time. The movie itself seems to be caught, for just a moment, in a stuttering repetition. Matalusa remains closest to the camera, but the other miners, behind him, continue to sway their bodies slowly, like zombies, as the music fades. We cut to a conversation, people seated amid the e-waste. One of the miners asks: "Help me to understand, one more time."

Minute 77

Neptune and Matalusa are seated side by side under a tree. Neptune tries to answer the miner's question, speaking of the need to change our actual practices. Memory rephrases this, adding that "Neptune has been generous in sharing her experience, but even she's not clear how it occurs." Conversation continues among the miners, focusing on their exclusion by the exploiters. "We mine, but don't own what we dig." Memory argues with some of the miners as they struggle to define terms and express their situation as accurately as possible. One of the most beautiful things about *Neptune Frost* is the ease and elegance with which it shifts between music and dancing and

FIGURE 15 Neptune Frost *directed by Saul Williams and Anisia Uzeyman* © *Kino Lorber 2021. All rights reserved.*

conversation, and dramatizes opposing arguments without insisting on a single conclusion, but also without dismissing its concerns into vagueness. The miners here, and Africans in general, are continually being exploited by the West, but it is important to analyze, as carefully as possible, the particular forms that this exploitation takes. And so one mode of presentation is displaced and replaced by another, all adding to the general impression that the movie gives. In its overall duration, *Neptune Frost* has a real density and depth; yet each individual moment is articulated lightly and clearly.

Minute 78

As Elohel joins the conversation, continuing to define the way that exploitation and extraction work, we also start to hear a drumming motif on the soundtrack. Neptune leans her head back and closes her eyes. More instruments are added to the soundtrack. The conversation fades out as Neptune's inner vision and audition replace what is objectively going on. We see distorted scan lines, first juxtaposed over Neptune's face and then filling the screen with a reddish or pinkish tint. The music gets more dissonant, electronic sparks fly, and electronic text flashes intermittently on the screen, as it previously did in Minute 61. I can only capture a few written phrases, most notably "ERASURE OF BLACK WOMEN." While the dissonant music of Neptune's vision continues on the soundtrack, on the image track, the actual world finally fades back in; Neptune remains in a sort of trance, and Matalusa looks at her with concern.

Minute 79

The music gets softer but doesn't entirely fade. Now the screen is tinted blue instead of pink-red. The camera is above the seated people, and we see them move in slow motion. We see Memory from behind and above, but she looks upward until her eyes make contact with the camera. We next see Neptune, sitting and consumed with her vision. Then we see Matalusa lowering his gaze. We return to Memory as she moves her head back down again. All this is shown to us in a state of suspension, as if the characters have fallen into a kind of hypnosis—or better, as if we, the viewers, had been so hypnotized. Both the other characters in the movie and we, the spectators, are somehow drawn into the space of Neptune's inner imagination. This is conveyed through something like what I would like to call, following Pier Paolo Pasolini, the "free indirect point-of-view shot"—which is to say, the visual, cinematic equivalent of the novelistic technique of free indirect discourse (Pasolini 2005). We see Neptune's abstracted blankness not only reflected in the faces of Memory and Matalusa but also taken up by the camera itself, as it pauses and shows us, from an oddly abstract and nearly impossible angle, with a bluish tint to everything, and with a drum 'n' bass track playing in the background, the bodies of all three characters as they sit motionlessly in a sort of circle. Finally, the suspension ends, and we cut to a shot with naturalistic lighting: a close-up of Memory's face, in profile, looking left. The next shot shows us Neptune, still in a trance, her eyes closed and her head leaning back against a wall. She opens her eyes and looks about in slight confusion.

Minute 80

As the privileged moment continues, the next shot brings us back to Memory in profile as she gently says to Matalusa: "Maybe you should take her [Neptune] back to rest." The camera moves to show us hands: both Memory and Matalusa grab Neptune's hands with their own and help her get onto her feet. This might be the moment to note that Matalusa now has painted fingernails, in contrast to the usual codes of masculinity. Everything blurs a bit; all we can see from this camera position is the swirling of the characters' clothing. The focus clears, and we see a bit of e-waste: something that looks

FIGURE 16 Neptune Frost *directed by Saul Williams and Anisia Uzeyman* © *Kino Lorber 2021. All rights reserved.*

like a large speaker box lodged against the trunk of a tree. Next, we see Neptune speaking enigmatically to Matalusa as he holds her and helps her walk back to their hut: "Memory stored in a cloud . . . Terabytes in C-major . . . First Nation sweat ceremony in a spaceship." And then, most strikingly: "To imagine hell is privilege." I think that we must take this statement as being directed to us, the audience watching the film, even though Neptune murmurs it to Matalusa within the diegesis. We are in a privileged position as we learn from the film about the cycle of extraction, production, use, obsolescence, and abandonment of the very technical devices without which we would have no access to it. As Neptune enunciates this sentence, she and Matalusa enter their hut, and the screen goes black for a moment. Now they are inside; as we have seen before, it is relatively dark, with computer monitors pulsing in bluish tints on the wall behind them. Neptune continues to speak of technological destruction as her hands tenderly caress Matalusa's face.

Minute 81

We are still inside Neptune and Matalusa's hut, with close-ups of their two faces and a computer monitor pulsing with colorful abstract patterns on the wall behind them. Neptune warns of machines "projecting destruction." Then she stops speaking but continues to caress Matalusa's face. As the camera circles slowly around them, they lean in and kiss one another; then they intimately hug. The monitor behind them still pulses with color, and we hear eerie electronic sounds. Neptune looks toward the camera and extends her hand, middle finger raised in a "fuck you" gesture, just as Matalusa did in Minute 76. As before, the screen immediately starts to glitch. The electronic noises pulse more loudly as the screen dissolves into metamorphosing abstract patterns, purple, red, and orange. There's a pulsing grid written across the screen, lines of code running downward on the left and right sides, and an amorphous orange cloud in the middle.

Minute 82

Through all the static, we see a television screen with the same white female newscaster as in Minute 61. She reports: "MYSTERIOUS HACKER MARTYRLOSERKING CONTINUES TO ELUDE AUTHORITIES." A version of this statement is also printed on the television screen. The newscaster disappears, fading back into the pulsing glitch patterns that fill the screen, though we still hear additional bits of her reporting on the soundtrack. The hack has affected "HUNDREDS OF MILLIONS OF SMARTPHONE USERS ACROSS THE OCCIDENTAL WEST." The screen excitingly pulses with disruptive energy; it is as if the movie itself is enacting the processes that it recounts. After a cut, putting an end to the visual glitches, the image of the newscaster now appears on a hexagonal wireless device, such as we have seen

FIGURE 17 Neptune Frost *directed by Saul Williams and Anisia Uzeyman* © *Kino Lorber 2021. All rights reserved.*

before, held in a hand. On the soundtrack, the electronic noise is replaced by a melody played on an mbira (the same motif that we previously heard in Minute 47). The camera pulls back, and in the nighttime darkness we see the miners listening to the broadcast. Their faces and shoulders are now covered in glitter. We also see Memory sitting among them. As the camera roves through this group of people, Psychology starts to wonder about the effectiveness of the hack: "These are games! It changes nothing. This is poetry!" He advocates using the hack to make an attack, to disrupt the Western economy, to hold it hostage: "Why not make a demand?" As Psychology speaks, the screen remains relatively dark; the camera roves among the group, some of whom are dancing, others of whom are just listening. Glimmers of light illuminate peoples' faces in chiaroscuro.

Minute 83

Psychology continues to speak. Finally, Memory answers him. She warns of the dangers of retaliation by the West, with its powerful weapons. "We power systems more effectively than we destroy them." Africa is the power source for the Western world; this is its strength, but it also means that it cannot destroy things as effectively as the West continually does. As for poetry, "it can help impart understanding. Understanding is all that is missing." Psychology responds in turn by noting that it may not be enough to just "recognize the pattern in the coding." He evokes all the Black bodies that have been destroyed, kidnapped victims drowned in the Atlantic during the slave trade, refugees seeking safety drowned in the Mediterranean today. The camera continues to rove around the entire group of people, some of whom are listening, and others of whom are dancing. The dark, slightly out-of-focus cinematography, with the mbira still playing on the soundtrack, provides a backdrop for the debate. I think that *Neptune Frost* asks us to take both sides of this argument seriously. Though some critics have accused the film of being overly didactic, I think they are wrong. The film combines dialectical debate with various sorts of atmosphere and anchors abstract arguments in situations of lived experience. In the present case, it is clear that poetry is not, in any immediate sense, politically efficacious. But perhaps we need to think and to act beyond mere immediacy. We might recall Neptune's voice-over in Minute 27, when she says of her own gender transition: "Maybe you're asking yourself WTF is this? Is it a poet's idea of a dream?" Poetry allows us to break free of the tyranny of binary gender. Along similar lines, Memory insists that we need "sharing thoughts, critiques, meditations, poetry" in order to survive and in order to be capable of further acts of resistance.

Minute 84

The discussion continues, as does the blurry background ambiance, with vague body shapes and music. Neptune joins the discussion, offering a kind of synthesis to Psychology's thesis and Memory's antithesis. Neptune points out that the Authority, and the Western powers behind it, want to turn the people into "robots," working automatically, without adequate pay, or even without pay at all. But such a robot "is dependent on human spirit to come to life. . . . One little Black girl algorithm brings it to life." Nobody has any further answers to this. Instead, the camera continues to linger on the ambiance. The same mbira music continues, but now it includes vocals. More and more people are dancing, their bodies illuminated in chiaroscuro, barely standing out from the surrounding darkness. One of the most powerful things about *Neptune Frost* is the wide diversity of visual textures, and regimes of lighting, among which it modulates. Some of these textures are naturalistic, some are vividly patterned, and some are garishly discordant and digital.

Minute 85

The screen is almost entirely dark, with only the barest glimmers of light momentarily visible, as the last of the music from earlier fades out. Then there is a cut to daytime: the camera pans over all the miners spread out on the ground, asleep; this is similar to what we saw in Minute 67. All is silent, except for the chirping of birds greeting the new day. Then the eerie electronic motif that we hear whenever anyone comes to the invisible barrier and enters the refuge starts to play. A man approaches through the clearing. He is wearing an army camouflage vest over a purple shirt and pants, with a metal disc in which computer microcomponents are embedded hung over his chest. Like the police confronting the student protesters, he wears a face mask and holds a machine gun. The miners are awakened, and they jump up in alarm. The man stands there, menacing them with the gun. A voice confronts him: "Innocent?" He is startled as he turns toward the voice (which is also toward the camera) and takes off his face mask so that we can now recognize him as Innocent, the man who tried to pick up Neptune earlier.

Minute 86

Memory walks into the frame and stares at Innocent. Then she stands by him, looks around at all the others, and introduces Innocent to them. Innocent is Memory's brother. He stands there impassively, then walks away with her. The miners are suspicious and displeased; they don't know what to do. Psychology says that the army must be near, and it will arrest them all. He wants to leave: "I'm going now." But Elohel immediately asks him, "Going where?" She adds that "if a soldier's here, the army is right behind. It's too late." She tells them about her previous encounter with the army: "when they cut off my arm, they left me for dead." Now we know why she has a prosthetic arm. But she recovered and came to (or founded) the refuge.

Minute 87

Elohel continues to speak: "I'm not running anymore. If it's over, it's over. We harm nobody here." It is true that the people of Digitaria are minding their own business and keeping apart from the rest of the world. But we should also remember the massive hack that was triggered all across the network by the mere coming together of Neptune and Matalusa; this is what the powers that control the outside world will not forgive. We cut to the darkness of Memory's hut. Innocent sits there motionless, with his eyes closed. On the soundtrack, we hear bird and animal cries and a low electronic rustling and rumbling. The camera pans over Innocent, over the miscellaneous pieces of e-waste, including circuit boards and binary code (numbers in base 2), that festoon the hut, and finally to Memory, who also sits in meditation, with her eyes closed and without moving.

Minute 88

After ten more seconds or so of continuing meditation, Memory opens her eyes, and the background electronic soundscape of mumbled words and distorted percussion suddenly cuts off. In the ensuing silence, Memory starts to question Innocent in a whisper: "What did you do?" He replies, offscreen, that "I didn't know." She continues to question him, with anguish, but still whispering, as the camera moves in toward her: "How could you not know? Has disguising yourself in the uniform of a soldier diminished your sensibilities?" In another reverse shot, as the camera moves very slowly around him, Innocent replies yet again that "I didn't know." Memory is still distressed; the movie cuts back to her as she tells him: "It was the Motherboard." This implies, I think, that Neptune is an avatar of the power of the digital. We cut back to Innocent as Memory asks him, reproachfully: "Did you need to know? . . . Was gender so crucial to your desire for intimacy? . . . Are you justified in attacking strangers who do not fulfill your unwarranted desires?" Innocent feels ashamed and cannot answer. The camera circles slowly around him as he hangs his head, followed by a cut back to Memory. We are in a moment of suspension. Memory's questions have an enormous weight, because they bring together so much that has happened over the course of the film, as well as because of the gravity that is produced by the slow shot-reverse shot editing in near darkness. Everything depends upon this quiet exchange. We realize more acutely than before how the utopian refuge of Digitaria, hidden deep in the forest, works as an answer to—or at least as a refuge from—all the terrible circumstances that we have witnessed in the outside world: the exploitation of labor for minerals, the sexual coercion and repression, the reign of normativity, and the Authority's dictatorship, including its crackdown upon the protesting students. Innocent is not violent or evil, but in his visit to Digitaria, as before in his wooing of Neptune, he nonetheless embodies and enacts a passive acquiescence in these bad conditions, which allows for their perpetuation. (Is this the reason for his name? Innocent is not himself willfully evil; he is not an exploiter. But this only means that he knows not what he does.)

Minute 89

We are still inside the darkness of Memory's hut. Innocent knows that he cannot answer Memory's questions and reproaches. Memory walks over to him and embraces him, cradling his head in her arms. The camera, close to their heads, moves in a slow part-circle around them. It is clear, from this embrace, that Memory truly loves Innocent, but she also knows that she needs to stop him from interfering with Neptune and with Digitaria. The silence between Memory and Innocent is long and drawn out, interrupted only by barely audible birdsong from outside the hut, as the camera slowly circles around them. Memory says to Innocent, quietly but firmly: "I asked you to stay on the path with me. And you refused." Mbira music with vocals starts playing softly on the soundtrack. Memory continues: "Now I must insist that you leave." At first Innocent jumps up and tries to protest. But Memory is firm: "Now," she says for a second time. Much of *Neptune Frost* is crammed full with words and music and lush images of life, but the slowing-down and suspension here, with the darkness and near-silence of the hut, is as eloquent and emotionally expressive as anything else in the film.

Minute 90

We see Innocent from behind as he stands for a moment in front of the hut and then walks out of the encampment. Neptune sees him and runs away in alarm. Then she stands by the wall of a hut and nervously watches him go; she is still poised to start running at any moment. The wall behind her is filled with yet more e-waste: the backs of televisions and monitors. There is more mbira music, supplemented with vocalizing, on the soundtrack, until it is drowned out by ominous electronic dissonance. We cut back to Memory, who is still sitting in the dark inside her hut. She starts talking to Elohel, who stands just outside the entrance to the hut. "It's not what you think," Memory says, "my brother is not the Authority, he is not a soldier. The uniform is a disguise." Elohel simply asks her, then, "Why?" Memory tries to explain the social causes of Innocent's normative masculinity, which oppresses him, but which he is unable to imagine an escape from: "Because they were born boys, and raised to uphold an idea of themselves that will not sustain them." This is the fate that Neptune escaped, but within which Innocent remains trapped. *Neptune Frost* is extraordinary to me, for the way that it expresses so much with so little, evoking an entire world situation from a few gestures and a few lines of dialogue.

Minute 91

Memory continues speaking of her brother's failures. Men like him, she says, "are priests at their own funeral." Psychology comes by and worries about what can be done. Memory tells him that she has sent her brother away; she stands up and comes to the entrance of the hut. She tells Psychology that she needs to speak to the entire group and asks Elohel to "go wake Matalusa and the Motherboard." As the mbira music resumes on the soundtrack, we cut to a shot of Neptune, wearing the wire-mesh mask that we only previously saw at the very start of the film, in Minute 2, walking by herself through the underbrush, away from the camp. Why is she leaving? Is this her response to seeing Innocent? The others are all gathered together, outside in the clearing, arguing about what they can do and whether they should stay and fight or leave to escape discovery. Memory arrives; they exchange the "Unanimous Goldmine" greeting, and they fall silent as she starts to address them.

Minute 92

Memory speaks, closely facing the camera, while all the others surround her and attend to her words. She talks of the rhythms of nature and of their place, as human beings, within it. We are like birds, she says, witnessing everything that happens. This includes both political injustices and orderly natural events. "We see it all." But as she speaks, there are cuts to shots in which the camera peers upward, through the branches of the trees, to a helicopter flying far overhead and outlined with green and red lights. Memory goes on to say that "we are hunted and honored, targeted and tethered," admitting that their treatment by the outside world has not been good. But she reminds them that "through it all, we have survived." Still, we cannot help realizing that safety is by no means assured. The helicopter flying overhead seems ever more ominous.

Minute 93

Memory continues to speak, envisaging "potential openings for new possibilities and greater and greater harmonies." But the miners are skeptical. "Why do you sing this old song when the soldiers are at our door?" She replies that "there are no soldiers coming," and furthermore, "even if they did, as long as the Motherboard is with us, we are protected." The Motherboard, of course, is Neptune herself, but we have already seen (though Memory and the others do not know this yet) that Neptune has departed from the encampment. Perhaps Memory overidealizes digital technology when she assures the miners that "technology is only a reflection of us." She fails to take account of the way that, when we shape things external to ourselves, whatever we have shaped then shapes (or misshapes) us in return. Memory says that Digitaria is itself a "gateway," in the same way that traditional African drums are a gateway to other realms. But of course, she admits, "the drum is nothing without the drummer." Who owns the technology that emerges out of the soil of Africa and the labor of Africans? This is the problem that Memory does not envision clearly enough when she exhorts everyone, in line with what we have heard throughout the movie, that "it's time we beat the code." This is entirely the right thing to do, but it might not be enough.

Minute 94

Elohel and Matalusa come running up to tell everyone that Neptune has disappeared. Nobody in the encampment saw her leave. We have seen her, however, wearing her elaborate headdress, walking through the underbrush in Minute 91. Memory claims that Innocent is "Ultra-Magnetic," but without any explanation of what this means. We cut to a brief shot of the bird Frost, once again flying at the left edge of the frame. This is followed by shots of Innocent walking away through the forest, reaching the invisible barrier that protects Digitaria, and passing through it to leave. Neptune, hiding in the underbrush and still wearing her headdress, watches his departure. We return to the encampment; Memory tells the others that she learned from Innocent that "the signal from the Motherboard was traced here. The Authority is working with European and US intelligence to avoid suspicion." Everyone groans; this certainly means that soldiers are coming.

Minute 95

Memory tries, without success, to convince the others that they are still safe. She speaks of how they have all followed their dreams to come to Digitaria and of the power of "love and music" to realize those dreams. Memory is my favorite character in *Neptune Frost*, but here she seems to be losing the thread, as her ideals (which are also the film's ideals) come under violent attack by the military (or by the Authority). We cut back and forth between Memory's ever-more-frantic efforts to explain and extreme close-up shots of Neptune in the underbrush, wearing her mesh mask and warily stooping down; on the soundtrack, we hear a dissonant electronic drone. Neptune looks around as the sounds of airplanes and explosions flood the soundtrack and the earth begins to shake. In a series of extremely quick cuts, we see the encampment in chaos, plus a shot from a bomb's point of view as it falls rapidly toward the encampment. We hear sounds of the attack—whooshing and explosions—as we once again see a bird flying high overhead. Then we see Neptune spinning around disoriented, trying to keep her balance, with motion blur obscuring her image, as more intense explosion sounds ripple through the soundtrack, and as smoke rises from the ground behind her.

Minute 96

The camera remains fixed on Neptune, her back to us as she stares at a distant scene of smoke and devastation. On the soundtrack, we hear continuing explosions, as well as birds chirping. There is a cut to a close-up of Neptune's head and face, encased in the mesh mask. Things quiet down for a moment, but then the sounds of the attack return. Now we see

FIGURE 18 Neptune Frost *directed by Saul Williams and Anisia Uzeyman* © *Kino Lorber 2021. All rights reserved.*

an entirely black screen, as the sounds of the attack continue. The sounds die away, and we see an out-of-focus shot of flames licking into the screen from below, with trees and leaves, profiled against the sky, slowly coming into focus in the background. The screen darkens again, lights into a close-up shot of flames, this time accompanied by the sounds of burning, then darkens again. There are no shots of actual explosions or of any sort of direct destruction. Doubtless, Williams and Uzeyman did not have enough of a budget for special effects. But the resulting indirection is quite effective, both thematically and emotionally. The Authority and the Western forces that back it are ultimately a nullity. They have no creative force of their own. All their power has been expropriated from the soil and the people of Africa, from minerals like coltan and from uncompensated human labor. As Memory said back in Minute 83, the people who have fled to Digitaria, and others like them, "power systems more effectively than we destroy them." But the Authority and the Western powers behind it are only able to efface and to destroy. Once the bombs have ravaged Digitaria, nothing is left, so there is nothing for the film to show us. This indirection also makes it easier for us to preserve in our minds the utopian vision of Digitaria, rather than allowing it to be overwhelmed by a spectacle of its destruction. The revolution has failed, but *Neptune Frost* leaves us with strong impressions of what was accomplished and of what still remains possible. A triumphalist movie would not make sense to us because the forms of oppression detailed in the film still continue to exist and to control the world with overwhelming power. But at the same time, the film's tragic narrative conclusion does not exhaust or efface the images and sounds of the preceding hour and a half. We are left with a vivid sense that other arrangements of life and technology are possible and that these have the power to disrupt and transform the contemporary ruling order. In the typology of the Marxist sociologist Erik Olin Wright, the film offers us the combination of *interstitial* and *symbiotic* metamorphoses of power: those that are built independently, in the gaps or interstices of the social order, and those that adopt the tactics and technologies of the social order as a way of pushing against them and modifying or inverting them (Wright 2010).

Minute 97

The final moments of the film remain melancholy and mournful, however. We alternate between shots of flames and shots where Neptune speaks while the frame is entirely dark. "What do you know of love? Of ruins beneath and before? Of fear?" Then Neptune's face in its mask and her upper body are silhouetted by the flame-filled sky. Elegiac or funereal music plays on the soundtrack as the screen continues to alternate between dimness and total darkness. Neptune continues to speak in voice-over; in spite of what has happened, she says, "I'm closer to birth than I am to death." There is more to come; this is not an ending, but a point from which we may begin all over again. Faint glimmers of flames are all that we can see as the funereal music continues. But we do not forget what we have seen and heard for an hour and a half of screen time prior to the attack.

Minute 98

More funereal music, more glimmering shots of flames. We can barely see Neptune walking in the darkness. We still hear her voice-over, or inner monologue, however: "What is mine? Dreams?" For a moment, we glimpse the crescent moon in an otherwise dark sky. More airplanes fly overhead, with green and red lights. Neptune repeats what she said at the very beginning of the film: "I was born in my 23rd year."

Minute 99

More darkness, more funereal music. We hear staticky transmissions from the helicopters: "AFFIRMATIVE. THE TARGET WAS DESTROYED." We can barely see Neptune in the darkness. Her image glitches, as earlier in the film. We hear the sound of what might be an electronic video device being turned off. But Neptune's body, facing us, is still faintly visible; she is no longer wearing the headdress. We start to hear drums on the soundtrack, and then an image slowly resolves out of the darkness: the drummers from Minutes 5 to 7 are once again playing, although this time in the darkness.

Minute 100

The drummers continue to drum in the darkness, now accompanied by vocals. They are all dressed in blue. We see a dancer way in the back, also dressed in blue, accompanying

FIGURE 19 Neptune Frost *directed by Saul Williams and Anisia Uzeyman* © *Kino Lorber 2021. All rights reserved.*

their rhythms. The camera holds still, though at one point the image glitches. The destruction of the realm of Digitaria does not negate the basic status of digital technology. This technology is still imperfect, and it is always bound to remain so. It originates from the earth and from the human labor that extracts it and gives it form. Both the powers and the glitches of this technology can be turned against the closure that its masters seek to enforce.

Minute 101

There are another couple of screen glitches, and the sounds and images of the drummers cease. The credits begin, over an image of the crescent moon with an aura around it. Military planes occasionally fly by. On the soundtrack, we hear nighttime sounds of birds chirping, together with soft electronics on the soundtrack. There's another glitch, followed by an image of Neptune, barely visible in the darkness. She speaks directly to us, in English, and with electronic distortion: "My truth is encrypted, and yours is easy to read. So what do you need to know about me? That I continue to exist?" And after another brief glitch: "I am the MartyrLoserKing. You build walls, but no firewalls to protect you from those who burn like candles, whose necks you can chop a million times, but still burn bright and stand." Neptune's rebellion cannot be squelched because it remains "encrypted": it persists, in hidden form, always ready to rise up and effloresce again, no matter how many times it has been stamped out and erased. This is the message of hope that *Neptune Frost* leaves us with. There's another electronic glitch, and the final credits resume, over music at a higher volume that repeats and elaborates themes from earlier in the film. I am ready to watch *Neptune Frost*, right from the beginning, all over again.

WORKS CITED

Abel, Mark (2014). *Groove: An Aesthetic of Measured Time*. Leiden: Brill.
Advanced Refractory Metals (2024). "Tantalum Capacitor Characteristics and Applications." https://www.refractorymetal.org/tantalum-capacitor-characteristics-applications/.
Althusser, Louis (1976). *Essays in Self-Criticism*. Trans. Grahame Lock. New York: Verso.
Bey, Hakim (2003). *T.A.Z.: The Temporary Autonomous Zone, Ontological Anarchy, Poetic Terrorism*, 2nd edition. Brooklyn: Autonomedia.
Bloch, Ernst (1986/1959). *The Principle of Hope*. Three volumes. Trans. Neville Plaice, Stephen Plaice, and Paul Knight. Cambridge: MIT Press.
Burton, Edson (2022). "When Traditional Myths and Afro-futurism Combine: An Interview with Neptune Frost Director Saul Williams." *The Bigger Picture*, October 26, 2022. https://www.the-bigger-picture.com/articles/when-traditional-myths-and-afro-futurism-combine-an-interview-with-neptune-frost-director-saul-williams/.
Champion, David (2019). "Australian Resource Reviews: Tantalum 2019." Commonwealth of Australia (Geoscience Australia). https://www.ga.gov.au/scientific-topics/minerals/mineral-resources-and-advice/australian-resource-reviews/tantalum.
Chang, Dustin (2022). "Interview: NEPTUNE FROST, Saul Williams and Anisia Uzeyman on Their Afrofuturist Musical." *Screen Anarchy*, June 1, 2022. https://screenanarchy.com/2022/06/interview-neptune-frost-saul-williams-and-anisia-uzeyman-on-their-afrofuturist-musical.html.

WORKS CITED

Connor, Will, and Rich Cooper (2025). "Weird Afrofuturism: The Sonic FX of Saul Williams and Anisia Uzeyman's *Neptune Frost*." Forthcoming in *Science Fiction Studies*.

Daniels, Robert (2022). "Making a Revolution: The Afrofuturist World of 'Neptune Frost'." *IndieWire*, November 11, 2022. https://www.indiewire.com/features/general/neptune-frost-behind-the-scenes-1234781524/.

Deleuze, Gilles (1986). *Cinema 1: The Movement Image*. Trans. Hugh Tomlinson and Barbara Habberjam. Minneapolis: University of Minnesota Press.

Deleuze, Gilles (1989). *Cinema 2: The Time-Image*. Trans. Hugh Tomlinson and Robert Galeta. Minneapolis: University of Minnesota Press.

Deleuze, Gilles (1990). *Logic of Sense*. Trans. Mark Lester. New York: Columbia University Press.

Deleuze, Gilles, and Felix Guattari (1987). *A Thousand Plateaus*. Trans. Brian Massumi. Minneapolis: University of Minnesota Press.

Deleuze, Gilles, and Felix Guattari (1994). *What is Philosophy*. Trans. Hugh Tomlinson and Graham Burchell. New York: Columbia University Press.

Derrida, Jacques (1978). *Writing and Difference*. Trans. Alan Bass. Chicago: University of Chicago Press.

Doane, Mary Ann (2002). "Technology's Body: Cinematic Vision in Modernity." In Jennifer M. Bean and Diane Negra (eds.), *A Feminist Reader in Early Cinema*, Durham: Duke University Press, 530–51.

Dwek, Joel (2021). "Les Maitres-Tambours du Burundi." https://www.200worldalbums.com/post/burundi-les-maitres-tambours-du-burundi-les-maitres-tambours-du-burundi.

ECM Records (2018). "The Art Ensemble of Chicago and Associated Ensembles." https://ecmrecords.com/product/the-art-ensemble-of-chicago-and-associated-ensembles-art-ensemble-of-chicago/.

Filmmaker Staff (2022). "The Camera Movements Were Almost Choreographed to Amplify the Ensemble Feeling, the Dances and the Musicality of That Universe: DP Anisia Uzeyman on *Neptune Frost*." *Filmmaker Magazine*, January 23, 2022. https://filmmakermagazine.com/112958-anisia-uzeyman-neptune-frost-sundance-2022/.

Flaxman, Gregory, ed. (2000). *The Brain Is the Screen: Deleuze and the Philosophy of Cinema*. Minneapolis: University of Minnesota Press.

Foucault, Michel (1998). "Different Spaces." In James D. Faubion (ed.), *Aesthetics, Method, and Epistemology: Essential Works of Foucault, 1954–1984, Volume 2*. Trans. Robert Hurley. New York: The New Press, 175–85.

Gates, Marya E. (2022). "Female Filmmakers in Focus: Anisia Uzeyman and Saul Williams on Neptune Frost." *Roger Ebert .com*, May 31, 2022. https://www.rogerebert.com/interviews/female-filmmakers-in-focus-anisia-uzeyman-and-saul-williams-on-neptune-frost.

Global Health Justice (2023). "Missionaries of Hate: U.S. Christian Right Group Enflames Homophobia in Uganda." https://depts.washington.edu/globalhealthjustice/1120-2/.

Graham, Ruth (2023). "What the Latest Investigations Into Catholic Church Sex Abuse Mean." *The New York Times*, June 2, 2023. https://www.nytimes.com/2023/06/02/us/catholic-church-sex-abuse-investigations.html.

Haraway, Donna (1991). *Simians, Cyborgs, and Women: The Reinvention of Nature*. London: Routledge.

Hoffman, Jordan (2022). "*Neptune Frost* Features Bold Colors—and Bolder Ideas." *AV Club*, June 1, 2022. https://www.avclub.com/neptune-frost-review-saul-williams-anisia-uzeyman-1848986774.

Jameson, Fredric (2005). *Archaeologies of the Future: The Desire Called Utopia and Other Science Fictions*. New York: Verso.

Keogan, Natalia (2022). "Revolutionary Song: Saul Williams and Anisia Uzeyman on Their Afrofuturist Musical, *Neptune Frost*." *Filmmaker Magazine*, Spring 2022. https://filmmakermagazine.com/114090-interview-neptune-frost-saul-williams-anisia-uzeyman/.

Kickstarter (2018). *Neptune Frost Kickstarter 2018*. https://www.kickstarter.com/projects/saulwilliams/neptune-frost.

KIno Lorber (2022). "*Neptune Frost* Press Notes."

Laughery, Jeremy (2025). "'It's Not What I See, But What I See Through': Queer Afrofuturism and AfroSurrealism in *Neptune Frost*." In DuEwa M. Frazier (ed.), *Introduction to Afrofuturism: A Mixtape in Black Literature & Arts*, London: Routledge, 129–40.

Leonard, Lana (2023). "Rachel Maddow Traces Anti-LGBTQ Legislation in Uganda to Activists in Arizona." GLAAD, May 3, 2023. https://glaad.org/rachel-maddow-traces-anti-lgbtq-legislation-uganda-activists-arizona/.

Lévi-Strauss, Claude (2021). *Wild Thought: A New Translation of La Pensée sauvage*. Trans. Jeffrey Mehlman and John Leavitt. Chicago: University of Chicago Press.

Lucier, Aurielle Marie (2024). "In the Open Air: Saul WIlliams on Breathing, Reading, and Resisting." *Scalawag*, September 3, 2024. https://scalawagmagazine.org/2024/09/in-the-open-air-saul-williams-on-breathing-reading-and-resisting/.

Marcks, Iain (2022). "*Neptune Frost*: Revolution in Rwanda." *American Cinematographer* 103:9 (September), 48–50.

Moylan, Tom (2014/1986). *Demand the Impossible: Science Fiction and the Utopian Imagination*. New York: Peter Lang.

Ndanezerewe, Dieudonné (2024). "News of Rich Mineral Reserves in Burundi Forest Reserve Sparks Debate." *Mongabay*, October 10, 2024. https://news.mongabay.com/2024/10/news-of-rich-mineral-reserves-in-burundi-forest-reserve-sparks-debate/.

Neuberger, Joan (2019). *This Thing of Darkness: Eisenstein's Ivan the Terrible in Stalin's Russia*. Ithaca: Cornell University Press.

Ngema, Zee (2022). "Interview: 'Neptune Frost' Is Here To Make You Question Everything You Think You Know About Film." *Okayafrica*. https://www.okayafrica.com/interview-neptune-frost-film-review/.

Obenson, Tambay (2021). "Neptune Frost: Saul Williams Confronts Status Quo with East African Cyber Musical." *IndieWire*, July 17, 2021. https://www.indiewire.com/features/general/neptune-frost-saul-williams-cannes-1234650362/.

Ojewale, Oluwole (2022). "What Coltan Mining in the DRC Costs People and the Environment." *The Conversation*, May 29, 2022. https://theconversation.com/what-coltan-mining-in-the-drc-costs-people-and-the-environment-183159.

Pasolini, Pier Paolo (2005). "The Cinema of Poetry." In *Heretical Empiricism*. Trans. Ben Lawton and Louise K. Barnett. Washington DC: New Academia Publishing, 167–86.

Powell, Jim (2021). "British Cotton and the American Civil War." January 25, 2021. https://jim-powell.net/2021/01/25/british-cotton-and-the-american-civil-war/.

Rodney, Walter (2008/1972). *How Europe Underdeveloped Africa*. New York: Verso.

Searles, Jourdain (2021). "*Neptune Frost*: Film Review | TIFF 2021." *The Hollywood Reporter*, September 21, 2021. https://www.hollywoodreporter.com/movies/movie-reviews/neptune-frost-tiff-2021-1235017758/.

Sobchak, Vivian (2004). *Carnal Thoughts: Embodiment and Moving Image Culture*. Oakland: University of California Press.

Tham, Xuanlim (2022). "Neptune Frost, the Afrofuturist Musical Imagining Life Beyond Capitalism." *AnOther Magazine*, November 3, 2022. https://www.anothermag.com/design-living/14495/neptune-frost-afrofuturist-musical-anisia-uzeyman-saul-williams-interview.

Vourlias, Christopher (2021). "Saul Williams on Mad Dash to Bring His African Sci-Fi Musical 'Neptune Frost' to Cannes." *Variety*, July 16, 2021. https://variety.com/2021/film/global/saul-williams-neptune-frost-1235010586/.

Wikipedia (2024a). "Coltan Mining and Ethics." https://en.wikipedia.org/wiki/Coltan_mining_and_ethics.

Wikipedia (2024b). "Work Song." https://en.wikipedia.org/wiki/Work_song.

Wikipedia (2024c). "Hacktivism." https://en.wikipedia.org/wiki/Hacktivism.

Wikipedia (2024d). "LGBTQ Rights in Rwanda." https://en.wikipedia.org/wiki/LGBTQ_rights_in_Rwanda.

Wikipedia (2024e). "Motherboard." https://en.wikipedia.org/wiki/Motherboard.

Williams, Eric (1994/1944). *Capitalism and Slavery*. Chapel Hill: University of North Carolina Press.

Williams, Maya (2022). "The Importance of Direction in Saul Williams and Anisiya Uzeman's Neptune Frost." *Black Girl Nerds*, June 1, 2022. https://blackgirlnerds.com/the-importance-of-direction-in-saul-williams-and-anisia-uzeymans-neptune-frost/.

Williams, Raymond (1978). "Utopia and Science Fiction." *Science Fiction Studies* 5:3 (November), 203–14.

Womack, Ytasha L. (2013). *Afrofuturism: The World of Black Sci-Fi and Fantasy Culture*. Chicago: Lawrence Hill Books.

Wright, Erik Olin (2010). *Envisioning Real Utopias*. New York: Verso.

Rodney, Walter (2008/1972). *How Europe Underdeveloped Africa*. New York: Verso.

Searles, Jourdain (2021). "*Neptune Frost*: Film Review | TIFF 2021." *The Hollywood Reporter*, September 21, 2021. https://www.hollywoodreporter.com/movies/movie-reviews/neptune-frost-tiff-2021-1235017758/.

Sobchak, Vivian (2004). *Carnal Thoughts: Embodiment and Moving Image Culture*. Oakland: University of California Press.

Tham, Xuanlim (2022). "Neptune Frost, the Afrofuturist Musical Imagining Life Beyond Capitalism." *AnOther Magazine*, November 3, 2022. https://www.anothermag.com/design-living/14495/neptune-frost-afrofuturist-musical-anisia-uzeyman-saul-williams-interview.

Vourlias, Christopher (2021). "Saul Williams on Mad Dash to Bring His African Sci-Fi Musical 'Neptune Frost' to Cannes." *Variety*, July 16, 2021. https://variety.com/2021/film/global/saul-williams-neptune-frost-1235010586/.

Wikipedia (2024a). "Coltan Mining and Ethics." https://en.wikipedia.org/wiki/Coltan_mining_and_ethics.

Wikipedia (2024b). "Work Song." https://en.wikipedia.org/wiki/Work_song.

Wikipedia (2024c). "Hacktivism." https://en.wikipedia.org/wiki/Hacktivism.

Wikipedia (2024d). "LGBTQ Rights in Rwanda." https://en.wikipedia.org/wiki/LGBTQ_rights_in_Rwanda.

Wikipedia (2024e). "Motherboard." https://en.wikipedia.org/wiki/Motherboard.

Williams, Eric (1994/1944). *Capitalism and Slavery*. Chapel Hill: University of North Carolina Press.

Williams, Maya (2022). "The Importance of Direction in Saul Williams and Anisiya Uzeman's Neptune Frost." *Black Girl Nerds*, June 1, 2022. https://blackgirlnerds.com/the-importance-of-direction-in-saul-williams-and-anisia-uzeymans-neptune-frost/.

Williams, Raymond (1978). "Utopia and Science Fiction." *Science Fiction Studies* 5:3 (November), 203–14.

Womack, Ytasha L. (2013). *Afrofuturism: The World of Black Sci-Fi and Fantasy Culture*. Chicago: Lawrence Hill Books.

Wright, Erik Olin (2010). *Envisioning Real Utopias*. New York: Verso.

INDEX

Abel, Mark 11
absolute survey 67
abstract value 8
afterlife 4
all-too-common binary 37
Althusser, Louis 63
Art Ensemble of Chicago 9
Authority 45–6, 81, 84, 88

Berkeley, Busby 10
binary crime theory 20
binary gender 46, 81
Bloch, Ernst 9
bodily metamorphosis 30
breath 32
Bresson, Robert 30
bricolage 18
bricoleur 50
Burundi 2, 6

call-and-response 55, 56, 63, 72
camera movement 28, 30, 49
Caravaggio 12
chthonic power 37
coltan mining 6, 7, 18, 73
computer technology 56
Connor, Will 45, 46
contestation 50
Cooper, Rich 45, 46

corporeal embodiment 72
cross-modal perception 21
cyberpunk 35

Daniels, Robert 64
Deleuze, Gilles 9, 22, 30, 54, 67
Democratic Republic of Congo 6
digital devices 14
digital technologies 33, 37, 50, 87, 93
Digitaria 11, 16, 19, 28, 29, 31, 33–5, 37, 44, 50, 54, 57, 67, 73, 83–5, 87, 88, 90, 93

e-waste 14, 50, 51, 55, 74, 77, 83, 85
economic exploitation of Africa 37
Eisenstein, Sergei 15, 54
elegiac/funereal music 91
expressive totality 63

Foucault, Michel 50
free labor 19
French New Wave 20

Godard, Jean-Luc 20, 61
Guattari, Felix 54, 67

INDEX

Haraway, Donna 73
heterotopia 50
high-technology capitalist world 73
Hoffman, Jordan 51

I-FI 67
Isheja, Cheryl 3, 32

Kayirebwa, Cécile 47
Kickstarter 1
King, Martin Luther 1, 2

landscape 32, 33
Laughery, Jeremy 3
Les Maitres-Tambours du Burundi 9
Lévi-Strauss, Claude 18, 50
liberation 9, 18, 51, 53
lines of flight 54
Lorber, Kino 1

marriage 43
Martyr Loser King (2016) 1, 58
masculinity 77
The Matrix Reloaded (2003) 58
mbira music 49, 80, 81, 85, 86
Melendez, Tanya 35
Mizero, Cedric 35
Muciyo, Rebecca 34

Neuberger, Joan 15
Ngabo, Elvis 3, 32
Niyongabo, Trésor 45
not-yet 9

out-of-focus cinematography 80

pan-African syncretism 33
Pasolini, Pier Paolo 76
Powell, Jim 7
printed circuit board (PCB) 27

Rwanda 2, 6, 9, 18, 33, 43

Searles, Jourdain 12
Sobchack, Vivian 21
soundtrack 7, 13–14, 20, 23–4, 27, 32, 41–5, 49, 53, 62–3, 66–8, 72, 76, 79–80, 83, 85, 86, 88–9, 91–3
space 30, 50, 61, 76
syncopation 11

tactile space 30
tantalum capacitors 6
technological landscape 36
Two or Three Things I Know About Her 61

Umuhire, Eliane 29
Uzeyman, Anisia 1, 9, 10, 12, 29, 33, 35, 43, 54, 64, 65, 90

Vlady, Marina 61
voice-over 3–6, 8, 23, 32, 53, 58, 61, 62, 66, 67, 81, 91

Western thought 20
Williams, Eric 7
Williams, Saul 1–2, 4, 7, 9, 11, 15, 18, 20, 29, 32, 33, 35, 43, 46, 58, 64, 90
world system 7, 14
Wright, Erik Olin 90